The Nailsworth and Stroud Branch

by
Colin G. Maggs

THE OAKWOOD PRESS

British Library Cataloguing in Publication Data
A Record for this book is available from the British Library
ISBN 0 85361 559 4

Typeset by Oakwood Graphics.
Repro by Ford Graphics, Ringwood, Hants.
Printed by Oakdale Printing Company Ltd., Poole, Dorset.

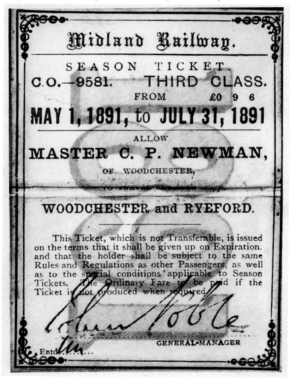

A Woodchester to Ryeford first class season ticket, 1891.

Title page: Class '4F' 0-6-0 No. 44045 leaving Dudbridge for Nailsworth on 5th October, 1962. The point lever for altering the junction turnout is beside the front wheel of the engine. The signal box has been removed but its toilet still stands. *W. Potter*

Front cover: '4F' class 0-6-0 No. 44264 is seen with the branch goods in Dudbridge yard in March 1964. *C.J. Gammell/Colour-Rail*

Rear cover: '4F' class 0-6-0 No. 44167 in Nailsworth goods yard, 13th June, 1962. *Author*

Published by The Oakwood Press (Usk), P.O. Box 13, Usk, Mon., NP15 1YS.
E-mail: oakwood-press@dial.pipex.com
Website: www.oakwood-press.dial.pipex.com

Contents

Woodchester, view towards Dudbridge. Note the creosoted timber building on brick foundation. The tops of the level crossing gates are at the foot of the picture, 31st May, 1956.   *Author*

341.—STONEHOUSE AND NAILSWORTH.

Incorporated by 26 and 27 Vic., cap. 132 (13th July, 1863), to construct a line from Stonehouse, on the Bristol and Birmingham line of the Midland, to Nailsworth. Length, 5¾ miles. Capital, 66,000*l.*, in 20*l.* shares; loans, 22,000*l.* Extra land, one acre; compulsory purchase, two years; completion of works, four years. Arrangements with Midland, which is to work the line. Works in progress, and the line expected to be open in May or June.

No of Directors—6; minimum, 3; quorum, 3 and 2. *Qualification*, 1,000*l.*

DIRECTORS:

Joseph Cary, Esq., 49, Pall Mall, S.W.
Henry Hawes Fox, Esq., 68, Queen's Gardens, Hyde Park, S.W.
William Playne, Esq.

Captain Robert O'Brien Jameson, 60, St. James's Street, Piccadilly, S.W.
A. M. Flint, Esq.
George Ford, Esq.

Stonehouse & Nailsworth Railway details from
Bradshaw's *Railway Manual & Shareholders' Guide*, 1869.

Seal of the Stonehouse & Nailsworth Railway. It is now held in Stroud Museum.

Chapter One

The History of the
Stonehouse & Nailsworth Railway

Tucked under the scarp of the Cotswold Hills nine miles south of Gloucester lies Stroud. Not mentioned in the Domesday Book, by 1248 the settlement had been accorded the status of a vill [feudal township], becoming a parish in 1304. In mediaeval times Cotswold wool was mainly exported but during the reigns of Edward II and III, the importation of cloth was prohibited and English cloth manufacture increased until by Tudor times the export of cloth replaced that of wool. Stroud developed as the Gloucestershire centre for the manufacture of broadcloth, the River Frome and its tributaries providing water for fulling mills and dyeing. Mills lined the Golden Valley from Stonehouse to Chalford, the district producing West of England cloth which was arguably the best woollen fabric in the world. Although the industry achieved its greatest prosperity between 1690 and 1760, cloth manufacturers found their trade hampered by the high cost of road transport to ships at Gloucester or Bristol. It is recorded that in 1763 Daniel Ballard ran stage waggons from Stroud to both these ports, whilst the first London stage coach service from Stroud was the Stroudwater Flying Coach established in 1769 and making the journey three times weekly. By 1830 daily services were run to London, Bath, Birmingham, Bristol, Cheltenham and Gloucester.

The fact that the price of Midlands coal sold for 10s. 6d. a ton at Gloucester, or 11s. at Framilode on the Severn, had risen to between 19s. and 22s. by the time it reached Stroud, led to the demand for a canal. It was estimated that a waterway could cut the price to about 15s. a ton and construction costs would be recouped within a decade. The Stroudwater Canal Act was passed in 1730 making it one of the oldest canal schemes in the country, though local opposition from mill owners prevented the exercise of these powers. A new Act was obtained in March 1776, the Stroudwater Canal opening from the River Severn through to Stroud on 24th July, 1779. On 17th April, 1783 Royal Assent was given to the Thames & Severn Canal Act to extend the Stroudwater Navigation from Stroud to the Thames at Lechlade. This opened on 19th November, 1789, the inland port of Brimscombe facilitating the transfer of cargoes from Severn trows to Thames barges. The Thames & Severn Canal failed to develop as expected, mainly only supplying coal to industry.

The waterways enjoyed a virtual monopoly of cartage until the mid-1830s when a cloud appeared on the horizon, threatening the navigation proprietors. Directly the GWR Bill for a line from London to Bristol had been passed by Parliament, some enterprising citizens of Cheltenham produced the Cheltenham & Great Western Union Railway scheme for linking their town with the GWR at Swindon. To avoid impossible gradients the line was to pass through Gloucester and Stroud, then climbing through the Golden Valley. This railway was eventually opened on 12th May, 1845. Although some traffic was siphoned from the canal, matters were not as serious for the water carriers as they could have been because topography forced the railway to be at a higher level than the canal so it was unable to serve the mills by convenient direct sidings.

From Stroud a side valley led south-east to Horsley, Avening and Minchinhampton. Although Nailsworth was mentioned in a charter of about 740 as 'Neglesleag minor', until 1892 when it was made into a parish, Nailsworth was merely a part of the parishes of Horsley, Avening and Minchinhampton, this explaining the apparent haphazard character of the town centre today. The building of the Bath Road in 1780 helped stimulate growth. Its relatively isolated position made Nailsworth an ideal place for secret worship and from early in the 17th century when the Quakers first met, the place became famous as a Non-conformist centre, with a Baptist congregation of 700 in the 19th century. Non-conformists largely ran the town in the 19th century and first half of the 20th century, being responsible for bringing about parish status. Nailsworth's sturdy, independent, friendly character of today is largely attributable to this Non-conformist influence.

The growth of Nailsworth demanded transport facilities and in 1854 an advertisement read: 'An omnibus leaves George Commercial Inn at Nailsworth for the Railway Station, Stroud, twice daily . . . fare 6d., without luggage', whilst a rival ran three trips daily between Stroud and the Clothier's Arms, Market Street, Nailsworth. The people of Nailsworth hated factories as this form of employment took away their independence and it was only with the coming of machinery in 1870-1880 that home weaving ceased, early mills being little more than dwelling houses. Because there was no water transport, coal was difficult to obtain. The eventual coming of the railway to Nailsworth had a great influence on the town, putting it in real contact with the outside world for the first time. Apart from benefitting industry, children were able to attend schools and technical college in Stroud, those with wealthier parents attending Wycliffe College, Ryeford, a Non-conformist public school, one of its famous pupils being William A. Stanier whose father lived at Swindon and was William Dean's chief clerk.

The first railway to mention Stroud was the Stroud & Severn Rail Road, with C. Baker as surveyor, the promotional meeting being held on 24th September, 1824. It was to be a locomotive-worked railway from Framilode on the Severn, or Frampton on the Gloucester & Berkeley Canal, to Dudbridge where it was to bifurcate: one line proceeding through Stroud to Brimscombe Port and the other to Iron Mills, Avening. Rail road promoters asserted that the charge of 3s. 6d. a ton for the 7¾ miles along the Stroudwater Canal from the River Severn to Wallbridge, Stroud, was exorbitant, especially as owing to the adoption of steam engines as auxiliary power 'the immense extension of Coals and other Articles annually transmitted by the Canal is of late exceedingly increased'. The canal proprietors claimed that the distance from the Severn to Wallbridge was over eight miles and although the charge was indeed 3s. 6d., no additional payment was needed to Brimscombe. It further claimed that coal would have to be waterborne across the Seven from Bullo Pill Coal Pits and transhipped and, although there was no canal to Nailsworth, 'the roads are exceedingly good' and coals were carried cheaply. A railway was certainly not a popular solution only 10 principal manufacturers subscribing from the many hundreds of clothiers living in the district. Of a subscription totalling £50,000, those 10 only subscribed, £13,000 leaving £37,000 to be subscribed by strangers. The scheme proved abortive.

In 1845 the Wilts & Gloucestershire Junction Railway was proposed with A.M. Ross as Engineer. Leaving the Cheltenham & Great Western Union Railway at Cainscross it was to connect the manufacturing districts of Stroud, Nailsworth and Tetbury with the Great Western Railway at Thingley west of Chippenham, the line showing the additional advantage of improving communications between the North and South of England, the distance to Thingley being only 24 miles compared with 44 miles via Swindon and 50 miles via Bristol. A branch was planned to run to the Bristol & Birmingham Railway at Stonehouse. Lacking the support of landowners, this scheme too proved abortive. Another still-born scheme put forward in 1845 was the Gloucester & Southampton Railway, proposed to run through Nailsworth, Tetbury, Malmesbury, Devizes and Salisbury. In June 1854 a proposal for a railway from Stroud to Nailsworth was rejected, never getting beyond the Parliamentary Committee stage. Not unnaturally it was opposed by the turnpike trust and the preamble was not proved. Surprisingly the rejection was partly due to religious prejudice, a concept rarely figuring in railway history. The *Stroud Journal* of 17th June, 1854 reported a member of the Committee, H. Drummond, as saying, 'I should have supported this Bill only I find it would give greater facilities for attending a certain Roman Catholic chapel at Woodchester, and as I have pledged myself to resist the Pope, the devil and all his works, individually and collectively, I agree with the last two speeches'. Lord John Russell, a former MP for Stroud and Prime Minister from 1846 to 1852 said: 'If it would have tended to promote religious liberty, I would have supported it; but as the inhabitants of the district are primarily dissenters and are not interfered with when they abuse the Roman Catholics and Puseyites, what can they wish for more? I cannot give my consent to this undertaking'. E. Horsman, MP for Stroud, said: 'I have been there (Stroud) once or twice, but know nothing of the wants of my constituents; it is not necessary for a member to do so now. I agree with the former speeches'.

These events led to the following farcical letter appearing in the *Stroud Journal* of 17th June, 1854.

Stonehouse & Nailsworth Railway Bill before the House of Commons Railway Committee. Mr Serjeant Shine for the promoters: Mr Chairman and Gentlemen - I have the pleasing duty of bringing before you a Bill to connect the two most important centres of manufacturing interest, Stroud and Nailsworth in the County of Gloucester. That two such places can exist in one county will be a matter of surprise when I detail the amount of public spiritedness which they evince. I assure you, gentlemen, it is quite overpowering . . . The promoters of this measure propose to connect Stroud and Nailsworth by means of a railway, with branches to Woodchester and Forest Green, places which though of limited size, are yet of immense consequence - at least in the opinion of the inhabitants . . . There will be stations at Lightmill, the Fleece and Dunkirk. Statistics of traffic in this case will be quite needless. I believe two omnibuses run several times a day, but the women and cripples are their sole patrons, for, as I before assured you, the people in this district are so much in advance of this present age that 60 miles an hour only will suit them. My learned friend will urge the claims of those wretched machines to compensation in the event of the preamble being proved, (of which of course there can be no doubt); but I trust this committee will not be weak enough to give way to my learned friend's eloquence. The engineering difficulties are comparatively

The Stonehouse and Nailsworth Railway Company.

CAPITAL £65,000, in 3,250 SHARES of £20 each

LOCAL COMMITTEE.

WILLIAM PLAYNE, Esq., Longfords, Minchinhampton.

S. S. MARLING, Esq., Stanley Park, Stroud.

J. G. FRITH, Esq., The Highlands, Nailsworth.

A. M. FLINT, Woollen Cloth Manufacturer, Nailsworth.

ISAAC HILLIER, Provision Merchant, Newmarket, Nailsworth.

A. S. LEONARD, Woollen Cloth Manufacturer, Nailsworth.

CHARLES PLAYNE, Woollen Cloth Manufacturer, Dunkirk Mills, Nailsworth.

J. E. BARNARD, Woollen Cloth Manufacturer, Lightpill Mills, Rodborough.

GEORGE FORD, Mealman, Ryeford Mills, Stonehouse.

THIS Railway, which is about six miles in length is intended to connect the populous and important manufacturing district of Nailsworth, and the intervening localities, with the Bristol and Birmingham Branch of the Midland Railway at Stonehouse. Passing through Stonehouse and near the Ryeford and Ebley Mills to Dudbridge and Woodchester, it terminates at Nailsworth, where a Station suitable to the wants of the district will be erected. Passenger stations will also be constructed at Dudbridge and Woodchester, and goods sidings, in the vicinity of the most important mills, will be laid on.

It must be apparent to the residents in the locality that the best interests of the district have been consulted in the course selected, and the Promoters, believing that a connection with the Midland system of lines would, on the score of expense and other important considerations, be preferable to one with the Great Western Company, have entered into negociations with the former, which have resulted in a preliminary agreement for the fair working of the line and the use of the necessary rolling stock.

After careful inquiries and a full consideration of the resources of the district and the large amount of goods traffic to be accommodated, the Promoters have arrived at the conclusion, in which they are fortified by the great experience of Mr. Allport, the General Manager of the Midland Company, that, in addition to the increased facilities which will be afforded to the district by the line, a favourable return on the Capital to be invested may be confidently calculated upon.

Responsible Contractors are prepared to provide one-half of the Capital if required to do so, and it is to the district that the Promoters now appeal for Subscriptions, which will make up the remaining moiety and enable them to bring the enterprise to a successful termination.

Application, in the subjoined Form, should be addressed to any Member of the Local Committee, or to G. B. SMITH, Esq., Solicitor, Nailsworth.

To the Local Committee of the Stonehouse and Nailsworth Railway Company.

Gentlemen,

I hereby request you will allot me   Shares of £20 each in this undertaking, and I agree to accept the same, or any less number that may be allotted to me, and to execute the Subscription Contract when called upon to do so.

Name _____

Address _____

Occupation _____

Date _____

Share advertisement in the *Stroud Journal*, 10th January, 1867.

nothing, since there will be only three viaducts, two tunnels and six rather sharp curves. In any other county these might prove objectionable, yet in the hands of the originators of this railway they are mere gnat stings . . . The capital required for the undertaking will be forthcoming. I am informed that the musical portion of the communities will supply the notes, and taking all the borough, if there should not be 'tin' enough, it is certain that the preponderance of another metal will more than supply the deficiency.

Mr Nubren was engineer and he 'knew the neighbourhood well', so well in fact that he just walked over it and sketched the plans as he came up in the train: there were no difficulties in it . . . Mr Nubren then described in detail his plans to the committee, who expressed surprise at the sharpness of the curves; but the witness stated they were nothing to the curves on some of his lines - in fact he had discovered a method by which a train could turn round a corner, and he proposed it, but the Directors, not being scientific men, would not sanction the application for £500,000 with which to try the experiment.

Betsy Smith, Abigail Jones, and many others then testified how much better it would be for them to ride to work boxed up in a carriage and remain all day in the close atmosphere of a mill, rather than walk over the hills, or through the valleys, and inhale pure air.

Vanden Bosch opposing said:

I oppose this measure principally in the part of the Trustees of the turnpike roads, who are determined to run the watercart of their displeasure over the scheme - in other words to throw cold water on it. The way in which the engineering difficulties are met with by the promoters is very peculiar, and can only be accounted for by supposing that my learned friend has some interest in the undertaking. If he can bore a hill a successfully as he can a committee, I should say he would be a valuable man in making tunnels . . . The method of 'raising wind' must be one of my friend's 'capital' jokes.

After the announcement that the preamble was not proved, Colonel Sinthorp commented: 'I should think not it's absurd nonsense! A pack of lazy rascals! As if they could not walk to work the same as they used to!'

As Nailsworth was only served by road and mill owners felt a desperate need for a railway, a scheme for constructing a branch line from the Midland Railway (MR) at Stonehouse was deposited in 1862. A special feature of the proposed branch was serving factories with individual sidings, unlike the Great Western which merely served stations. A local committee was set up in January 1863 consisting of William Playne, Samuel Stephens Marling (the largest clothier in the district), J.G. Frith, Isaac Hillier (purveyor of pig products), A.S. Leonard, J.E. Barnard, George Ford and Charles Playne. The Stroudwater Canal opposed the scheme as the planned railway ran parallel with the canal between Stonehouse and Dudbridge posing a serious threat to its trade, but the only concession granted to the canal proprietors was a free transhipment siding at Stonehouse Wharf as compensation for the line passing through part of their property. John H. Taunton, manager of the Thames & Severn Canal had no confidence in the future of his canal unless it was converted into a railway. He advocated transferring wagons to pontoons at the wharf and floating them to wharves and mills as far as Brimscombe, even making suggestions of joint traffic arrangements with the GWR and MR, but these interesting proposals proved abortive.

Poster advertising cutting the first sod of the Stonehouse & Nailsworth Railway. This poster is now at the Stroud Museum.

The Act of Parliament received Royal Assent on 13th July, 1863, (26-7 Vict. cap. 132) giving powers to construct a line 5¾ miles in length from the MR at Stonehouse to Nailsworth, the authorised capital being £66,000 and loans of £22,000. Powers were granted to make arrangements with the MR to maintain, manage and work the line 'upon the usual terms of 50 per cent of the receipts'. The prime purpose of the line was, as James Allport, General Manager of the Midland stated, to connect Stonehouse with Nailsworth, chiefly for the benefit of the considerable cloth industry in that valley, Stroud being a secondary consideration. He added that the Midland had no wish to enter into competition with the GWR for Stonehouse to Stroud traffic - though we shall see that his company would shortly change its views and from the opening of the branch ran omnibuses from Dudbridge to Stroud.

The first meeting of the Stonehouse & Nailsworth Railway (SNR) was held in the Subscription Rooms, Nailsworth on 19th October, 1863, the Directors being William Playne, Chairman; A.M. Flint and George Ford, all local men; Joseph Cary of Pall Mall; Henry Hawes Fox, Hyde Park and Capt Robert O'Brien Jameson, Piccadilly. The contract for constructing the line was let to Messrs Watson, Overend & Co., the ceremony of turning the first sod being carried out at Nailsworth on 22nd February, 1864, the two Nailsworth cannon firing before daybreak and continuing periodically until late at night. The sod was turned by the Rt Hon. E. Horsman MP in a meadow belonging to Messrs P.P. & C. Payne of Egypt Mill, close to the spot where Nailsworth station was to be built.

The *Stroud Journal* of 27th February, 1864 reported: 'It is well understood to be the first step in an extension on through Tetbury, Malmesbury and Chippenham, and both Great Western and Midland companies are fighting for powers to construct the contemplated line'. The day was declared a general holiday, all shops and factories being closed from noon. A large gas-illuminated star was fixed to the cloth factory of Messrs Flint & Sons to celebrate the occasion.

Mr W. Playne, as Chairman, and Mr G.B. Smith, as Secretary, have worked most indefatigably, and successfully in obtaining the line and to their exertions the success of the project is in great measure due . . . Flags, banners, mottos and evergreen devices decked the houses in profusion and by midday thousands of visitors had flocked into the town, making it fuller and gayer than it has perhaps ever been before . . . At one o'clock the stream of people in the streets tended towards the Subscription Rooms where a procession was formed for proceeding to the scene of the ceremony. At the head marched the band of the Stroud Rifle Corps, with several banners. Then came Mr Horsman MP for the borough, who had been invited to perform the ceremony of the day, accompanied by the officials of the line and a large number of the principal gentlemen of the neighbourhood.

The procession stopped just outside the Rooms to be photographed, an operation which caused considerable delay. It then moved on to the gay sounds of the bands, swelling as it went, and amidst an immense concourse of spectators lining the road on the whole route to the field where the sod was to be turned.

Silence having been obtained, the Revd W.L. Mills, Incumbent of Nailsworth, offered a prayer invoking a prayer invoking the Divine Blessing on the undertaking. Mr G. Bruce, the Engineer, then advanced and presented Mr Horsman with an

Cutting the first sod of the Stonehouse & Nailsworth Railway on 22nd February, 1864. Note the cannon used to celebrate the event on the left and right.   *Mrs Makemson*

Dinner ticket for meal celebrating cutting the first sod.

STONEHOUSE & NAILSWORTH RAILWAY.

(CUTTING THE FIRST SOD.)

DINNER TICKET.

SUBSCRIPTION ROOMS, NAILSWORTH,

MONDAY, FEBRUARY 22, 1864,

at THREE o'Clock.

Admit *Mrs A. E. Smith*

Procession *at One o' Clock,*
(from the Subscription Rooms.)
Ceremony *at Two o' Clock.*

elegant silver shovel, the gift of Mr J. Watson, one of the contractors. Mr Horsman then proceeded to turn the sods which had been made ready, throwing them a short distance in a good humoured manner which highly amused the crowd. Some of these sods were picked up and carried off by the possessors, who will probably preserve them as mementos.

A dinner for about 120 was held in the Subscription Rooms.

There were other enjoyments provided for the holiday-keepers . . . At four o'clock commenced a series of rustic sports, which comprised donkey and foot-racing for prizes, and other pastimes which caused much merriment . . . At six o'clock the illuminations were lit up and the town was ablaze with light. At seven o'clock a torchlight procession proceeded up Nailsworth hill, and the effect was very pretty . . . So ended a happy day which passed off without mishap and was of the greatest pleasure to all concerned.

All but one of the townsfolk kept sober, one man telling the police that he had been to a children's party but found the tea 'too strong'.

The capital was soon raised, £24,000 by shareholders and £20,000 by the contractor. On 30th August the Stonehouse & Nailsworth Railway shareholders were told that the contractors had pushed forward the work with 'utmost vigour' and that more than two-thirds of the land had been handed over to them; it was anticipated that the line would be completed in May 1865. Half the fencing had been erected; five-eighths of the earthworks moved and half the masonry of bridges and culverts erected, whilst a large proportion of the rails had been delivered. George Barclay Bruce (knighted 1888) was Engineer to the SNR from its inception, some of his previous appointments being Engineer to the Royal Border Bridge, Berwick; the Calcutta section of the East Indian Railway and the Midland & Great Northern Railway. In March 1865 he reported that despite the bad weather, the line ought to be opened during the summer. A landslip had taken place above Frogmarsh cutting north of Woodchester, the sliding clay slope causing the foundations of a house above the cutting to slip. In the early stages of its excavation the householder used to take to bed with him all the necessary tools to open his bedroom door in the morning. The slip ceased only when Bruce drained off the springs from the higher ground.

Men constructing the railway did not escape injury. On 7th September, 1866 when the goods shed at Nailsworth was under construction, an end wall and archway fell, smashing the legs of White, a mason from the nearby village of Horsley, while his colleague Gardiner suffered spinal damage. Both were taken to Stroud Hospital. When they had arrived that morning the men noticed that the building had settled a foot during the night and, prior to the accident, had hoped to remove the stonework to prevent further sinking. The settlement had been caused by recent heavy rains damaging the foundations.

The line finished, Colonel Yolland on behalf of the Board of Trade made the following the report:

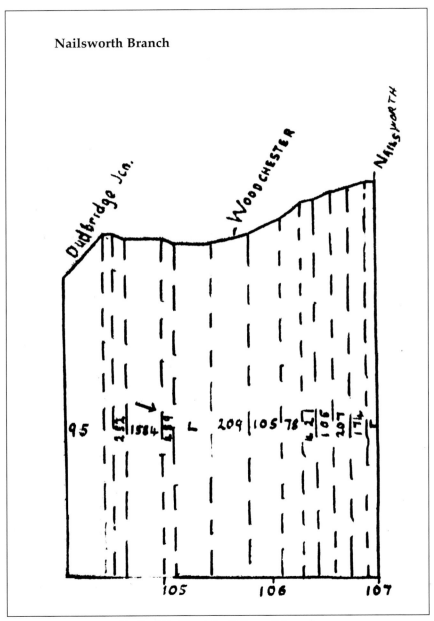

Gradient Profile of the Nailsworth branch.

Newcastle
8th December, 1866

Sir,

I have the honor [sic] to state for the information of the Lords of the Committee of the Privy Council for Trade, that, in obedience to your minute of the 28th Ulto. I have inspected the Stonehouse & Nailsworth Railway, which forms a Junction with the Birmingham and Bristol Section of the Midland Railway at Stonehouse, and extends to Nailsworth a length of 5 miles 58½ chains.

The line is single throughout with sidings at several stations, but the land has been purchased and the overbridges and masonry for the under-bridges has been constructed for a double line.

The width of the line at formation level is 18 feet; the gauge is 4 ft 8½ inches, and the width between lines, where there are two, is 6 feet.

The permanent way consists of a double headed rail that weighs 75 lbs per linear yard, in lengths of 24, 21 and 18 feet, fixed in cast iron chairs that each weigh 26 lbs, by means of compressed oak keys placed outside the rails. The chairs are secured to transverse sleepers by two iron spikes each 6 inches long and ⅞ in. diameter for each chair. The joints of the rails are fished with wrought iron plates 18 inches long, screwed together by four ⅞ inch bolts with nuts. The sleepers on the main line are of Baltic red wood 9 feet long by 10 in. x 5 in. rectangular. In the sidings, larch is used 9 feet long by 10 in. x 5 in. half round. The sleepers are placed at an average distance of 3 feet apart from centre to centre. The ballast is of gravel, and stated to be 12 inches deep below the under sides of the sleepers. The steepest incline is 1 in 75 and the sharpest curve has a radius of 20 chains.

There are 6 over and 14 under bridges - constructed with brick or stone abutments and with arched or flat tops, carried by cast or wrought iron girders. The largest span is that over a canal of 56 feet span, in which wrought iron girders are employed, supported on one side by brick abutments, and on the other by cast iron columns. The masonry and brick work is good - the iron girders are sufficiently strong by calculation and exhibited moderate deflections under a rolling load.

There are no authorised level crossings on the line.

Stations have been provided at Ryeford, Dudbridge and Nailsworth, and also a coal station at Woodchester.

The line is in fair order.

In making my inspection I noticed the following -

1. An engine turntable is in course of erection at Nailsworth station, but none has been provided at the junction at Stonehouse - and no station accommodation has been constructed at this junction, it having been intended to make use of the Midland station. This arrangement however, would render it necessary for all trains proceeding to or coming from Nailsworth to be shunted for about ¼ of a mile as the junction is situated about that distance from the station and this would be very objectionable. The proper arrangement would be to shift the Midland station up to this junction - at all events platforms with shelter &c must be provided for passengers at this junction proceeding to or coming off this railway. And a low signal is required to prevent trains from coming out of a siding east of the Midland lines between the junction and the station.

2. At the bridge over the canal, transoms and cross tie are required between the longitudinals that carry the rails - and some of the iron girders require to be bolted down on to the top of the cast iron columns.

3. Two of the over bridges, one at 4 m. 31 ch. and the other at 4 m. 69 ch. appear to be slightly shaken, and one of them is slightly out of form. These will require to be watched.

4. Several of the facing points require a second connecting rod, between switches: the lever handles for working the distant signals at Dudbridge station require to be shifted:

Midland Railway.

DERBY TO GLOUCESTER, BRISTOL, &c.
FEBRUARY, 1867,
AND UNTIL FURTHER NOTICE.

Trains do **NOT STOP** at the Stations marked with **SMALL** Figures unless marked thus ✳ where they are liable to stop for Water only

REDDITCH TO BARNT GREEN.

Miles	STATIONS	WEEK-DAYS										SUNDAYS			
		1	2	3	4	5	6	7	8	9	10	1	2	3	4
		Pass. and Goods	Pass. and Goods	Gds.		Pass. and Goods		Pass.	Pass. and Goods	Goods	Pass. and Goods	Pass.	Pass.	Pass.	Pass.
		a.m.	a.m.	a.m.		p.m.		p.m.	p.m.	p.m.	p.m.	a.m.	a.m.	p.m.	p.m.
	REDDITCH	8 0	9 55	11 10	..	2 5	..	3 35	5 15	6 45	8 5	7 0	10 10	5 10	8 50
3	Alvechurch	8 9	10 4	11 19	..	2 14	..	3 44	5 24	6 54	8 14	7 9	10 19	5 19	8 59
4½	BARNT GREEN ..	8 15	10 10	11 25	..	2 20	..	3 50	5 30	7 0	8 19	7 15	10 25	5 25	9 5

8 Train runs when required.

BARNT GREEN TO REDDITCH.

Miles	STATIONS	WEEK-DAYS										SUNDAYS			
		1	2	3	4	5	6	7	8	9	10	1	2	3	4
		Pass. and Goods	Pass. and Goods	Gds. and Coal.		Pass. and Goods		Pass.	Pass. and Goods	Goods	Pass. and Goods	Pass.	Pass.	Pass.	Pass.
		a.m.	a.m.	a.m.		p.m.		p.m.	p.m.	p.m.	p.m.	a.m.	a.m.	p.m.	p.m.
	BARNT GREEN ..	8 35	10 35	11 40	..	1 40	..	4 5	5 55	7 10	8 45	7 25	10 40	5 40	9 20
1½	Alvechurch	8 41	10 41	11 50	..	1 46	..	4 11	6 1	7 16	8 51	7 31	10 46	5 46	9 26
4½	REDDITCH	8 50	10 50	12 0	..	1 55	..	4 20	6 10	7 25	9 0	7 40	10 55	5 55	9 35

8 Train runs when required.

NAILSWORTH TO STONEHOUSE.

Miles from Nailsworth	STATIONS.	WEEK-DAYS.									
		1	2	3	4	5	6	7	8	9	
		Goods, &c.	Passenger	Engine	Passenger	Engine	Goods, &c.	Passenger and Goods	Engine	Goods, &c.	9 Train, see Page 52, Train 55.
		a.m.	a.m.	a.m.	a.m.	p.m.	p.m.	p.m.	p.m.	p.m.	
1	NAILSWORTH	7 30	9 40	10 18	11 45	12 50	2 0	5 10	6 53	9 20	..
1½	Woodchester	7 40	..	..	..	..	2 25	..	..	9 45	..
3	Dudbrige	7 47	9 48	..	11 53	..	2 50	5 20	..	10 10	..
4½	Ryeford	7 55	9 52	..	11 57	..	3 5	5 26	..	10 25	..
	Stonehouse Junction	..	..	..	..	..	..	..	..	..	..
5½	STONEHOUSE	8 0	10 0	10 30	12 5	1 5	3 10	5 35	6 5	10 30	..

STONEHOUSE TO NAILSWORTH.

Miles from Stonehouse	STATIONS	WEEK-DAYS									
		1	2	3	4	5	6	7	8	9	
		Goods, &c.	Engine	Passenger	Engine	Passenger	Goods, &c.	Engine	Passenger	Goods	9 Train, see page 45, Train 42.
		a.m.	a.m.	a.m.	p.m.	p.m.	p.m.	p.m.	p.m.	p.m.	
1	STONEHOUSE	8 30	10 1	10 40	12 6	1 15	3 30	5 36	6 10	7 45	..
1½	Stonehouse Junction	..	..	..	..	..	..	..	..	..	..
2	Ryeford	8 45	..	10 48	..	1 23	3 55	..	6 18	8 10	..
4½	Dudbridge	8 55	..	10 52	..	1 27	4 10	..	6 22	8 25	..
4½	Woodchester	9 10	..	..	..	..	4 30	..	..	8 45	..
5½	NAILSWORTH	9 15	10 13	11 0	12 20	1 35	4 36	5 48	6 30	8 55	..

Extract from the Midland Railway Working timetable of February 1867 showing the services on the Nailsworth branch.

buffers are required at the end of the line at Nailsworth and some little fencing to be completed near Ryeford station.

5. The sidings at several of the stations join the main line, beyond the control of the station signals. This is not of importance, while the line is worked, as I understand, (as) it is now proposed to be worked by a single engine - but in the event of that mode of working being changed, additional signals should previously be put up, to be worked by the signalman who has charge of the station signals. For the same reason some of the stations are partly constructed on gradients on which carriages would run by the force of gravity: and this is of no importance while there is only one train on the line at one and the same time. I have not received an undertaking from the company, concurred in by the Midland Railway Co. who are to work the line, with reference to the mode of working.

I have now therefore to report that by reason of the incompleteness of the works, the opening of the Stonehouse and Nailsworth Railway for traffic cannot be sanctioned, without danger to the public, using the same.

> I have the honor to be
> Your most obedient Servant
> W. Yolland
> Colonel

Bruce sent a letter to the Board of Trade dated 27th December saying that its requirements had been met - the platform at Stonehouse and the turntable at Nailsworth were completed, transoms laid on the canal bridge, signal handles altered at Dudbridge, connecting rods added to all points, signals erected at Stonehouse to control the siding and buffers installed at Nailsworth [remarkably quick work on the part of the company]. This leads to Colonel Yolland reinspecting the line on 4th January, 1867.

> Railway Department
> Board of Trade
> 5th January, 1867

Sir,

I have the honor [sic] to report for the information of the Lords of Committee of the Privy Council for Trade, that, in obedience to your minute of the 28th ulto, I yesterday reinspected the Stonehouse & Nailsworth Railway.

The overbridge at 4 miles 69 chains referred to in my report of the 8th ulto as being out of form, has been taken down and is to be rebuilt - and the whole of my requests detailed in that report have been complied with, except as regard the erection of an engine turntable at the junction with the Midland Railway at Stonehouse.

There will be no objection to this railway being opened for traffic without delay, if the Midland Railway Company who are to work the line, and are understood to be largely interested in it, will give an undertaking to the effect that they will run all their passenger trains on this branch line from Nailsworth to Gloucester where there is, I am informed, an engine turntable, until an engine turntable is put in at the junction at Stonehouse; but until such an undertaking is received. I have to report that the Stonehouse & Nailsworth Railway, cannot by reason of the incompleteness of the works, be opened for traffic without danger to the public using the same.

I should add that I have received a complaint on the subject of a level crossing at Stonehouse, which I will forward as soon as I am finished with some additional information and which I have asked for.

> I am
> W. Yolland
> Colonel

RAILWAY PLANT.

Stonehouse and Nailsworth Railway,
Stonehouse Station, Gloucester.

Re Contract Corporation Company, Limited.

BY ORDER OF THE OFFICIAL LIQUIDATOR,

Mr. WILLIAM FREEMAN,

(Proprietor of "Aldridges," St. Martin's Lane, London,)

WILL SELL BY PUBLIC AUCTION,

WITHOUT RESERVE,

ON TUESDAY, JUNE 18th, 1867, at 12 o'clock, at STONEHOUSE STATION,—

THE whole of the CONTRACTOR'S PLANT, which has been used in the construction of the Stonehouse and Nailsworth Railway, consisting of a

POWERFUL CYLINDER TANK LOCOMOTIVE;

SMALL PILE ENGINE AND MONKEY;

53 END TIP WAGGONS;

A LARGE QUANTITY of TEMPORARY RAILS;

TRAVELLING CRANE;

Twelve dobbin carts; hand and wheelbarrows; a number of permanent sleepers; many thousand feet lineal of planking; platelayer's levers; timber and stone drags; single and double-purchase crabs; portable forge; sheriff and pinch bars; a large quantity of chairs; fish plates; fang and fish bolts; temporary and permanent crossing blocks; cast-iron barrow wheels; round, twisted and square spikes; wrought and cut nails; drag; tip and dobbin chains; earth pick and beaters' heads; ratchet braces; screw jacks; taps and dies; many lots of quarry and plate-laying implements; scrap iron; and sundry other effects.

The lots may be viewed Two Days before the Sale, and Catalogues had of C. F. Kemp, Esq., the Official Liquidator, 8, Walbrook; Messrs. Linklater and Co., 7, Walbrook; M. Abrahams, Esq., 8, Old Jewry, London; on the Premises at Stonehouse Station; and of Mr. Wm. Freeman, "Aldridge's," St. Martin's Lane, London.

Advert for sale of contractor's plant at Stonehouse in *Stroud Journal* of 8th June, 1867.

G.B. Smith, the SNR Secretary, commented that he 'could not help expressing surprise that a short country line proposed to be worked by tank engines should be reported as unsafe for passenger traffic, when upon that system there is conducted in London the largest passenger service in the world'. On 26th January Smith promised to run engines of all passenger trains back to Nailsworth to turn until the table at Stonehouse was completed in mid-February and with this assurance the Board of Trade allowed the branch to open. It opened to goods on 1st February and to passengers on 4th February. Unusually for the period there was no formal ceremony organised by the railway company, though a large number of passengers travelled by the first train which left Nailsworth at 9.40 am, the engine being decorated with flags and evergreens. Crowds welcomed the train with 'enthusiastic acclamations'. Cannons were fired from High Beeches and from the Subscription Rooms at Nailsworth whilst in the evening bands paraded the streets. The opening of the railway led to the establishment of Nailsworth Market, first held on 19th March, 1867. The *Stroud Journal* of 8th June, 1867 listed for auction equipment used in constructing the line including 'a powerful cylinder tank locomotive, small pile engine and monkey, 53 end tip wagons, travelling crane and portable forge.

Nailsworth had second thoughts on having a celebratory dinner, the *Stroud Journal* on 25th January, 1868 reporting:

For some time past the idea has been entertained of holding a dinner amongst the officials employed on this railway in commemoration of the opening of the line, and it is now arranged to take place at the George Hotel on the evening of this day (Saturday) week, when the whole of the officers connected with the branch will assemble under the presidency of the promoters and Directors of the line. Already upwards of £10 has been promised towards the dinner.

On 5th July, 1867 Colonel Hutchinson inspected the newly-provided passenger station at and required a fence along the back of the platform. The *Stroud Journal* of 6th July reported:

A station at Woodchester on the Stonehouse and Nailsworth line, which opened for the first time on Monday last (1st July). All the trains will stop at the new station; particulars of which will be found in our timetables. The erection of the station is a great convenience to the residents of the neighbourhood, who have hitherto considered themselves slighted by the non-erection of a station when the line was constructed.

It is believed that the station at Woodchester was primitive, the following letter appearing in the *Stroud Journal* several years later on 14th March, 1874.

Woodchester Station

To the Editor of the *Stroud Journal*

Sir - Permit me for one moment, through the medium of your journal, to lay before the notice of the Directors of the Stonehouse and Nailsworth Railway the importance of having more suitable and decent waiting-room accommodation at the Woodchester station. This is the only station on the line which is not provided with the desirable accommodation, and I do not think it is the least important one, but even if it be it does not follow that the convenience and comfort of passengers should be in any way prejudiced thereby. From what I can ascertain, applications have been made to those in

An engraving of Rooksmoor Mills, taken from an old letter heading. *Author's Collection*

An engraving of Nailsworth Mills, with the station on the left.

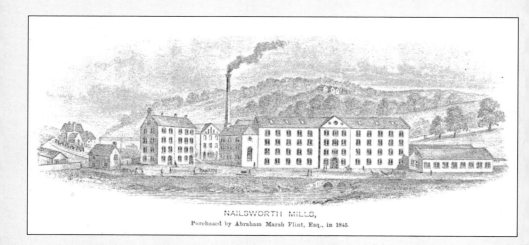

NAILSWORTH MILLS,
Purchased by Abraham Marsh Flint, Esq., in 1845.

authority, asking them to provide the accommodation I speak of, but up to now nothing has been done. Since the passenger and goods traffic on this branch have been combined, and the punctuality of the trains on this account cannot be guaranteed, it is therefore of the utmost importance that the comfort of the passengers should be carefully studied, for I myself have frequently had to wait (and others also have been obliged to wait) sometimes 20 minutes - sometimes even 30 minutes - exposed to damp and cold.

I have therefore undertaken to write this letter on behalf of the persons who are accustomed to travel from the fore-named station, trusting it will have the desired effect, and I feel that the good feelings of the Directors will at once prompt them to make arrangements for providing the accommodation which is absolutely necessary.

Yours faithfully
William J. Ford

The Grange,
Woodchester March 9th 1874

It is thought that the heated waiting room was built soon after this complaint was received.

Traffic earnings for the half-years ending December 1867 and June 1868 were as follows:

December 1867

	Gross Receipts			MR Working Expenses 50 per cent*			SNR Proportion 50 per cent		
	£	s.	d.	£	s.	d.	£	s.	d.
Coaching	786	7	1	393	3	6	393	3	7
Goods (less cartage)	1,063	14	9	531	17	5	531	17	4
Cattle	33	9	0	16	14	6	16	14	6
Mineral	206	14	6	103	7	3	103	7	3
Total	2,090	5	4	1,045	2	8	1,045	2	8

June 1868

	£	s.	d.	£	s.	d.	£	s.	d.
Coaching	713	6	11	356	13	5	356	13	6
Goods (less cartage)	885	4	4	442	12	2	442	12	2
Cattle	34	9	1	17	4	6	17	4	7
Mineral	150	19	3	75	9	7	75	9	8
Total	1,783	19	7	891	19	8	891	19	11

* Excluding amount for station accommodation at Stonehouse.

Although on the surface all appeared well, this was far from being the case. A financial crisis was looming. On 6th November, 1867 a deputation from the SNR approached the Midland Board to seek further financial assistance, but this was refused 'as they did not think under existing circumstances such would be a fitting step to submit to the Midland Proprietors'. Two days later the SNR pleaded to the MR that the first four months of its half-yearly earnings for 1867, namely £675 7s. 10d., be paid immediately in order to settle the debenture interest of £450. On 21st December C. Winterbotham was appointed Receiver.

An outside-frame 0-6-0ST arrives at Nailsworth in 1873. The message in the bottom left-hand corner reads 'Just arrived'.　　　　*C. Wells Collection*

0-6-0ST No. 2008 outside the engine shed at Nailsworth in 1873. The passenger loop can be seen at a higher level.　　　　*Revd W.V. Awdry*

The Midland found the financial position of the SNR an embarrassment when on 29th January 1868 a bill was filed by a landowner against the bankrupt SNR for payment of lands taken, the Midland being named co-defendant.

On 31st August the SNR Directors reported that because of trade depression preventing an increase in traffic, the company was in pecuniary difficulties. The Stroudwater Canal Company had successfully claimed damages for interruption of traffic and recovered a judgement. The 1863 Act had stated that if the passage of boats on the canal was impeded by a bridge being across it west of Ryeford, the canal company was entitled to £30 for every 24 hours' delay. The Act also stated that the bridge should not be less than 8 ft above the towpath and 12 ft above the surface of the canal, whilst the towpath should be 8 ft wide. As these measurements were infringed, to defray damages and costs the SNR was required to pay £1,060, though in the event this was not handed over until 1878. The opening of the SNR had serious repercussions on the Stroudwater Canal which found much of its traffic diverted to the new line. Paying its last dividend in 1922, the sale of water has enabled the company to survive to the present day.

The Midland kept the Nailsworth line open by constantly paying the SNR's debts, but in July 1869 Samuel Stephens Marling of Stanley Park and other unpaid landowners whose claims amounted to £7,000, applied to the Court of the Chancery to rescind their contracts for selling land and to restrain the Midland from working the line. This threat was successfully parried by the Midland's solicitors, Messrs Beale, Marigold & Beale and traffic continued, the MR still paying debts amounting to several thousand pounds. The only real solution was for the Midland to absorb the SNR for, having sunk so much capital in the line, the MR was loathe to let it close.

Negotiations for absorption began on 6th November, 1872 and finished on 5th July, 1877. The terms of the MR Additional Powers Act Vict. 41& 42 cap.96 of 17th June, 1878 were:

1. That the Stonehouse & Nailsworth Railway be vested in the Midland Railway 'in perpetuity', free from all encumbrances and liabilities.
2. That the Midland paid in cash £28,000, the amount of the debentures and £2,000 to clear the debts and liabilities of the SNR.
3. That the shares held by the Midland were to be cancelled and the MR pay an annual rent equal to three per cent on the remaining ordinary shares amounting to £40,940.

For the half-year ending 31st December, 1878 and the year ending 31st December, 1879 the MR paid the SNR a shilling rent and for the year ending 31st December, 1880 and all subsequent years £1,228 4s. 0d. The Receiver appointed by the Court of Chancery in the suits of Jewsbury v. the SNR and Spain v. the SNR was discharged. An important feature of the arrangements was that the Stroud branch was to be built without delay. Not building this line originally was a serious error of judgement. for in setting aside the Stroud branch as a 'secondary consideration', they were ignoring the fact that Stroud was the local centre and hence a generator of traffic. The SNR was dissolved in 1886 to become part of the Midland Railway.

Chapter Two

The Wiltshire & Gloucestershire Railway

A the first meeting of the SNR on 19th October, 1863 the Directors agreed that their scheme was incomplete unless extended to Stroud and also to Christian Malford, the latter place being between Swindon and Chippenham on the Great Western's London to Bristol line. They proposed that the extension be of mixed gauge to offer equal facilities to both the MR and GWR. S.S. Marling chaired a meeting at Stroud on 31st October, 1863 which supported the resolutions passed at a meeting at Tetbury five days earlier.

Two plans were deposited in 1863: The Gloucestershire & Wiltshire Railway running from Nailsworth to Christian Malford and having the same Engineer as the SNR, and the Wiltshire & Gloucestershire Railway with R.J. Ward as Engineer and running in reverse direction from Christian Malford to Nailsworth via Malmesbury and Tetbury, these towns not yet having their own railway. Inclines over the latter proposed line were to be easier than those of the existing Cheltenham & Great Western Union Railway, the ruling gradient being 1 in 75 compared with 1 in 60.

The following year an Act, 27-8 Vict. cap. 222 of 25th July, 1864 was passed to construct a mixed gauge line from Christian Malford to Nailsworth. Capital was to be £243,000 in shares and £81,000 in loans. It was to be broad gauge throughout with the option of mixed gauge in whole or part. The SNR and lessees were to give facilities for laying broad gauge from Nailsworth to Stonehouse (the MR's Bristol to Gloucester line was mixed gauge at this period), while reciprocally the SNR had powers to lay mixed gauge over the Wiltshire & Gloucestershire Railway (WGR). Powers permitted the WGR to have a joint station at Nailsworth with the SNR and working and traffic arrangements could be made with the GWR and MR. In order to protect local traffic on the SNR, the WGR was not permitted, without the consent of the former, to pick up and deliver to any other SNR station.

By 30 Vict. cap. 57 of 31st May, 1867 an extension of time for completion of work was granted until 25th July, 1872, this Act also allowing the division of shares into deferred and preferred types. The first Directors of the WGR were: Rt Hon. Thomas Henry Estcourt, Sir Richard Hungerford Pollen Bt (Chairman), the Rt Hon. Earl of Suffolk & Berkshire, Samuel Bendry Brooke, William Capel, Edwin Cook, Robert Stayner Holford, Samuel Stephens Marling and Walter John Stanton.

Under a Heads of Agreement dated 21st February, 1865 between the MR and the WGR, the former agreed to work the WGR as a continuation of the SNR. Christian Malford was not the final objective as was shown the following year when an Act was passed (28 & 29 Vict. cap. 338 of 5th July, 1865), for building the North & South Wiltshire Junction Railway from Christian Malford across the downland to the Berks & Hants Extension Railway (worked by the GWR) near Woodborough. The North & South Wiltshire Act allowed working agreements to be made with the MR and SNR. Directors were Samuel Stephens Marling, Walter Stanton, George Ford, William Playne, William Nicks, Alfred Selfe Leonard and William Crousden Tunstall.

402.—WILTS AND GLOUCESTERSHIRE.

Incorporated by 27 and 28 Vic., cap. 222 (25th July, 1864), to construct a line from Christian Malford to Nailsworth. Length, 23 miles. Mixed gauge. Capital, 243,000*l.*, in 10*l.* shares, and 81,000*l.* on loan. Working and traffic arrangements with Midland and Great Western.

Meetings in February and August.
No. of Directors—9; minimum, 5; quorum, 3. *Qualification, 500l.*

DIRECTORS :

Earl of Suffolk and Berkshire.	Robert Stayner Holford, Esq.
Sir Richard Hungerford Pollen.	William Capel, Esq.
Samuel Stephens Marling, Esq.	Samuel Bendry Brooke, Esq.
Right Hon. T. H. S. Sotheron Estcourt,M.P.	Walter John Stanton, Esq.
Estcourt House, Tetbury.	Edwin Cook, Esq.

Wilts & Gloucestershire Railway details from
Bradshaw's *Railway Manual & Shareholders' Guide*, 1869.

The Wiltshire Railway, authorised by 28 & 29 Vict. cap. 318 of 5th July, 1865 was to run to Pewsey, a few miles east of Woodborough, over Salisbury Plain to Idmiston on the London & South Western Railway (LSWR) six miles north-east of Salisbury. The Wiltshire Railway was authorised to make working arrangements with the LSWR and GWR. The Midland did not propose to work the North & South Wiltshire Junction Railway or the Wiltshire Railway. Its right to work the Wiltshire & Gloucestershire Railway was denied in 1866 by Captain Douglas Galton of the Board of Trade, who had been appointed arbitrator in pursuance of the 1863 Agreement whereby the MR and GWR agreed not to extend into each other's territory, or lease or work lines in the other's district. On Galton's decision being published, construction of the WGR ceased as the Midland Railway would have been unable to work it. The ceremony of cutting the first sod had taken place at Malmesbury on 1st July, 1865, the *Swindon Advertiser* reporting that the Countess of Suffolk & Berkshire turned it gracefully 'amidst cheers and music, the event being solemnised by an appropriate prayer from the Revd Canon Estcourt'. Today the ceremonial spade and barrow are displayed in the Athelstan Museum, Malmesbury. In 1869 receipts of the WGR were £13,674, the expenditure leaving a balance at the bankers of £2,244. The company was eventually dissolved in 1870.

Several other abortive suggestions were made for extending the SNR. The South Midland Railway was put forward in 1871 to run from Lydney, across the Severn to Berkeley Road and through Wotton-under-Edge to Malmesbury where the branch from Nailsworth was to join, the combined line continuing to a junction with the GWR at Wootton Bassett. It was planned to cross the Marlborough Downs and divide at Hungerford: one line proceeding to the LSWR at Andover, while the other served the same company at Basingstoke. The project proved abortive.

John H. Taunton, manager of the Thames & Severn Canal had no confidence in the future of his company unless it was connected with a railway. His previous experience had certainly qualified him to make comment as he had surveyed a number of railway routes, had worked with Brunel and served as district engineer in charge of constructing a section of the Oxford, Worcester & Wolverhampton Railway.

In 1866 the Thames & Severn Canal applied to Parliament for a connection with the SNR starting near Ebley and almost following the route of the extension to Stroud authorised in 1864, but with a station on the Upper Canal Wharf, this being part of a proposed through line to Oxford.

Taunton's proposal for a 24 mile-long line to the East Gloucestershire Railway at Fairford would have utilised the formation of the canal between Stroud and South Cerney, passing through the Sapperton canal tunnel on a single line. It would have provided a standard gauge route from South Wales to London and had the advantage of crossing the Cotswolds on a gradient of 1 in 120 instead of 1 in 60 of the Great Western's route.

Although the GWR and the LNWR engaged counsel to oppose the proposed line, it is significant that the MR did not, though it should be pointed out that outright sale of the canal to the MR was rejected by James Allport, MR General Manager. The Bill sought extensive running powers covering some 45 miles of other companies' lines and, William Henry Barlow, consulting engineer to the Midland, questioned by the Commons Committee as to the purpose of these powers, said that they were to enable the Thames & Severn Railway to work its own coal trains from the Forest of Dean to Oxford 'without break of gauge, or any change of engine, or any stop'. William Cawkwell and James Grierson, General Managers of the LNWR and GWR respectively, pointed out that even if the Thames & Severn supplied the entire Oxford market, coal traffic would only yield £7,000 a year and it seemed that the line was to be built as a threat to the GWR. The Commons passed the Bill, but it was rejected by the Lords.

The idea was not entirely forgotten and in February 1882 a Bill was introduced by Richard Potter, timber merchant of Gloucester and former Chairman of the GWR, for the conversion of part of the neglected and difficult-to-work portion of the Thames & Severn Canal into a railway which was to leave the authorised Swindon & Cheltenham Extension Railway (later the Midland & South Western Junction Railway (M&SWJR)) at Siddington and join the authorised MR line at Stroud. This scheme would have placed the Severn & Wye Railway on a short route to London since the Severn & Wye already possessed running powers to Nailsworth. However, the Bill was defeated by the Sharpness New Docks & Gloucester & Birmingham Navigation Company which also managed to secure the support of the Stroud Navigation, Wilts & Berks Canal, Severn Commissioners, Staffs & Worcs Canal and the Birmingham Canal Navigations. These canals enlisted the support of other waterway authorities and approached the Board of Trade telling Joseph Chamberlain, its President, that in their opinion Potter's proposal violated the Regulation of Railways Act, 1873. Chamberlain said he would oppose the Bill. Potter found Sir Daniel Gooch, Chairman of the GWR, ready to negotiate. On 11th May, 1882 the Great Western agreed to purchase Potter's Thames & Severn shares and as many of the other shareholders' as cared to sell. They also stipulated that Potter should pay the GWR the £2,000 he had received from the Midland Railway (*see Chapter Three*). A variation of Potter's scheme was put forward in July 1893 when the Severn & Wye Railway, with MR support, was contemplating building a short connection from Nailsworth to the M&SWJR at Cirencester to make a connection with the LSWR.

Chapter Three

The Stroud Branch

Although the Midland had disclaimed an interest in Stroud, by August 1864 the company had opened an office in the town and John Bradford, the MR agent, ran buses from this office to Stonehouse station, the return fare, without luggage, being 1s. 6d.

John Hunt, owner of two large cloth mills at Stroud, was in favour of the MR opening a branch to the town saying that his wool came from Hull and if a line was built it could come through by Midland Railway. Exports via Bristol would be eased as the existing practice was to send goods by road to Stonehouse before forwarding by rail. Hunt added that a rail link would enable him to use part of the output of Coalpit Heath collieries north of Bristol. Richard Grist & Son, flock manufacturer, said that a branch would obviate the change of gauge at Gloucester, at that time unavoidable because there was no alternative to the GWR. Edmund Boughton, an iron manufacturer of Birmingham, sent 100-150 tons of iron and tinplate to Stroud annually, it travelling to Gloucester by water and then onwards to Stroud by rail, whereas a standard gauge line to the town would have allowed him to send it by rail throughout.

With Bruce as Engineer, a plan had been deposited in 1863 by the SNR for building a branch from the authorised Nailsworth line at Dudbridge making a junction with the GWR north of Upper Ganicox in order that the GWR station could be used. A rival plan submitted by the Wiltshire & Gloucestershire Railway with Ward as Engineer, was for a line from Dudbridge to Stroud, bifurcating east of the Stroud the Stonehouse turnpike road, the branch proceeding either side of the Great Western line so that Dudbridge trains did not foul the GWR line with its 25 trains a day. In order to do this it was planned to pass under the GWR, forming an early instance of a burrowing junction. In 1864 Bruce submitted a modified plan, a ruling gradient of 1 in 85¼ replacing that of 1 in 60 and with a 40 ft deep cutting instead of a tunnel.

This was authorised by the SNR Act of 28 & 29 Vict. cap. 177 of 29th June, 1865. Capital was to be £35,000 in shares and £7,600 on loan, the MR being authorised to subscribe £35,000 to the NSR and having powers to appoint a Director on contributing a further £20,000. Provision was also made in the Act for working agreements between the MR, GWR and SNR companies. The GWR was allowed to call for broad gauge to be laid and could employ its clerks on stations. Richard Potter who owned the controlling interest in the Thames & Severn Canal, sold part of the canal wharf at Stroud to the MR for a station site. For this and for promoting the Bill to change part of the Thames & Severn into a railway, Potter received a personal gift of £2,000 from the MR.

In November 1865 and July 1866 the MR bought £10,000 five per cent preference shares and £25,000 ordinary shares on the undertaking that construction of the line would not be delayed and it was agreed that the £35,000 invested by the MR:

Shall be applied in the construction of the proposed extension . . . and also towards the cost of doing away with certain level crossings at Stonehouse Wharf over the road leading to Bridge End; and Mr Bird's private road leading to his mill and dwelling house, 100 horse drawn vehicles and 300 people on foot using the first crossing daily.

S.S. Marling had previously made complaints regarding the danger of these crossings.

On 3rd October, 1866 the Secretary of the MR wrote to the SNR calling attention to the fact that no progress had been made with the Stroud branch and reminding them that it was on a distinct agreement that the branch be at once proceeded with that the MR had advanced the cash.

One of the reasons for lack of progress was that SNR shareholders had no direct interest in building the branch to Stroud, the existing GWR line supplying the accommodation they required. Stroud tradesmen, however, were vexed that the business of the Nailsworth district should be diverted to Gloucester to which access was as easy as Stroud.

In 1871, owing to the death of Mrs Mansfield, the Fromehall estate at Stroud came on the market. Taunton, Engineer and Manager of the Thames & Severn Canal and the proponent of the Thames & Severn Railway suggested to the MR that it buy the estate with a view to building a branch from Dudbridge to Stroud. The suggestion was acted upon and land purchased for £8,100. In June and August 1875 more land was bought in the vicinity of the estate for £1,800. It took some time to acquire by private purchase other properties along the route, but this was ultimately done. On 5th July, 1877 a meeting with Sir Samuel Marling of Stanley Court resulted in the curve to Stroud east of Dudbridge station replacing a planned triangular junction to the west. On 6th August, 1880 the MR, practically unopposed, obtained Parliamentary powers, 43-4 Vict. cap. 146, to build a branch from Dudbridge to Stroud with a station on the Wallbridge Mill estate. On 12th July, 1882 the powers were amended by 45-6 Vict. cap. 130, the station being placed a little further northward nearer the Stroudwater Canal and the town, with the authority to build a road from Rowcroft to it. Meanwhile in July 1881 John Underwood on the Midland's civil engineering staff, prepared plans, specifications and estimates for the extension. On 31st October, 1882 nine tenders were received, that of Thomas Oliver of Horsham being accepted at £37,198 8s. 9d. Although this seems a very hefty sum for a single line branch only 1¼ miles in length, it involved a heavy cutting, embankment, viaduct and numerous bridges. Oliver started work about the beginning of 1883.

The *Stroud Journal* of 17th October, 1885 reported:

This mile of railway is now within measurable distance of completion, after nearly three expensive years of work. It is expected that goods traffic will be opened on the first of next month and passenger traffic on the first of January 1886. The goods station at Stroud is finished and the passenger station is commenced. At Dudbridge the new station accommodation is nearly complete, the requisite signal boxes are up and the permanent way has been laid over nearly the whole route. Many travellers on the Nailsworth branch have reason to hope that when the work is complete better time will be kept.

The passing loop and second platform at Dudbridge being complete, the Board of Trade inspection was carried out:

The Assistant Secretary	Railway Department
Railway Department	Board of Trade
Board of Trade	1 Whitehall
	London SW
	4th November, 1885

Sir,

I have the honr [sic] to report for the information of the Board of Trade, that, in compliance with the instructions contained in your minute of the 23rd ultimo, I have inspected the alterations at Ryeford and Dudbridge on the Nailsworth branch of the Midland Railway – a single line.

At *Ryeford*, where there is one platform only, the position of some points has been altered, and the signalling arrangements have been revised, being now carried out in a new Cabin containing 12 levers, of which 2 are spare.

At *Dudbridge*, where is the junction of a branch line to Stroud, now nearly complete, a passing loop and second platform have been constructed, and so new signal Cabins have been built.

Dudbridge sidings cabin at the back end of the loop contains 16 levers of which 2 are spare, and Dudbridge Junction Cabin at the East end of the loop contains 20 levers, of which 2 are spare.

In the former Cabin, Nos. 4 & 8 levers should be interlocked, and at the junction the facing points should be fitted with an additional appliance to prevent, in case of the failure of any of the connections, either Home signal from being lowered unless the points are lying in the proper direction.

Subject to the satisfaction of these requirements, I can recommend that the use of these new works may be sanctioned.

> I have the honour to be
> Your most obedient servant,
> F.A. Marindin
> Major

The extension to Stroud was opened to goods traffic on 16th November. On 6th March, 1886 the *Stroud Journal* wrote: 'This expensive piece of line is now within measurable distance of being opened for passenger traffic, a notice having been issued by the Midland Railway Company for the official inspection of the Dudbridge-Stroud line to take place within 10 days of Monday last'.

The Secretary	Railway Department
Railway Department	Board of Trade
Board of Trade	12th March, 1886

Sir,

I have the honour to report, for the information of the Board of Trade, that, in compliance with the instructions contained in your minute of the 3rd instant, I have inspected the Stroud Branch Railway and Deviation of the Midland Railway Company.

The new line is a single line on the 4 ft 8½ in. Gauge. It is about one mile 23.6 chains long. The steepest gradient is 1 in 70, and the sharpest curves have Radii of 9 and 10 chains. It joins the Stonehouse and Nailsworth Branch of the Midland Railway with a double junction and there is a loop line with sidings at Stroud, which is the terminal Station of the new Branch line. The line Junction points at Stroud are locked with an Annett's key. There are no signals at Stroud Station.

The permanent way consists of a bull-headed steel rail, that weighs about 83 lbs per lineal yard. It is fished and fixed with wooden keys in cast iron chairs that weigh about 50 lbs each. The chairs are fastened to transverse wooden sleepers with 2 wrought iron spikes and two treenails. The sleepers are 9 feet long, 10 x 5. There are 11 to each 30 ft rail. The 3 centre sleepers are about 3 feet part, and the rest are – two 2 ft 11 in.; two 2 ft 9 in.; and two 2 ft 3 in., and two 2 ft 2 in. apart, the latter are next to the rail joints. The line is well ballasted and well fenced.

There is a Viaduct over the river that consists of one brick arch, and a second Viaduct near Stroud Station that consists of 9 brick arches and one opening, over which the Railway is carried by cast iron girders on brick piers and abutments.

There are two bridges over the Railway which consists of brick arches, and one that has wrought iron girders on brick abutments.

One Bridge under the Railway consists of a brick arch and a second has wrought iron Girders on Brick abutments. The widest spans is 39 feet 4 inches.

These works have been well and substantially constructed. The iron Girders are sufficiently strong by calculation, and showed very moderate deflections when loaded.

There is also a small foot bridge over the Railway which carries a water pipe. The platform of the bridge is of wood and the piers are of brick.

A check rail has been placed round the 9-Chain Curve and the same should be done round the 10-Chain Curve.

Some loose ballast should be placed at the end of the safety points at the south end of the loop at Stroud Station to prevent an Engine that may over-run these points from going too far. Subject to these small requirements being executed, and to a satisfactory Undertaking as the proposed mode of working this single line being sent to the Board of Trade, I recommend the Board of Trade to sanction the line being opened for passenger traffic.

I was informed that it is intended to work the line with only one Engine in Steam or two coupled together.

I have, etc.
F.H. Rich,
Colonel R.E.

The *Stroud Journal* for 10th April reported:

We are informed that the new Midland line from Dudbridge to Stroud will be opened for passenger traffic on the first day of May. There will be eight trains daily each way. The report of the Local Government Inspector [sic] is satisfactory, the one alteration required, that of check rails over the Stroud viaduct, having been already complied with.

A fortnight later it announced:

A party of directors and officials visited Stroud on Wednesday afternoon (21st April), in the course of a three days' progress over the lines which form the western portion of the Midland Railway. They travelled in a handsome and convenient 'bogie' saloon drawn by a special engine, and during their half-hour's stay at Stroud, went all over the passenger and goods stations and their approaches. No date was fixed for the opening of passenger traffic. The rumour started recently by some irresponsible person, as to the opening on the first of May, is entirely without foundation.

Costing £13,000, including buildings, the station at Stroud was opened for passenger traffic without ceremony on 1st July, 1886. A slight collision occurred in the afternoon when a passenger train collided with a goods engine, no damage being done apart from the passengers receiving a severe shaking. Later in the day more passengers had a scare when an engine running round, backed too sharply on to the coaches. The inhabitants of Stroud welcomed the MR, John Libby, the Stroud historian recording in his *Twenty Years' History of Stroud, 1870 to 1890* that 'The Great Western in the face of competition, awoke to their true interest, viz., that of giving the public every facility for travelling; and it seems as if both the railways had doubled their passenger traffic . . . The people are not slow to avail themselves of improved locomotion, when liberally and cheaply provided'.

Passenger Bookings at Stroud

	GWR station			MR station	
Year	No. of passengers	Passenger receipts £		No. of passengers	Passenger receipts £
1868	49,957	8,773		-	-
1886	n/a	n/a		36,048 *	1,506 *
1887	n/a	n/a		77,818	3,507
1888	77,309	10,064		79,367	4,504
1889	81,482	10,783		81,877	5,104
1913	535,585 †	20,812		63,350	4,550

n/a = not available   * 6 months only, from opening of station 1st July.
† Railmotor service in operation. MR Passenger station expenses in 1913 were £415.

Motor bus competition started as early as April 1908 when Jeffrey & Co. of Nailsworth, commenced running a single-deck bus service between Nailsworth and Stroud, five buses each way daily undercutting the railway fares. Just prior to the withdrawal of passenger train services in 1947 the number of passengers carried annually was about 6,000.

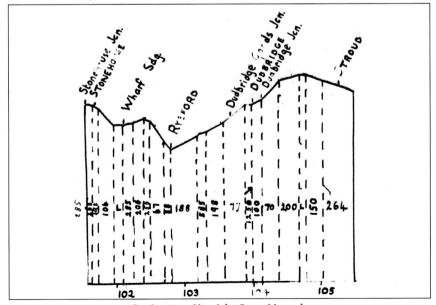

Gradient profile of the Stroud branch.

Courtesy Peter Smith

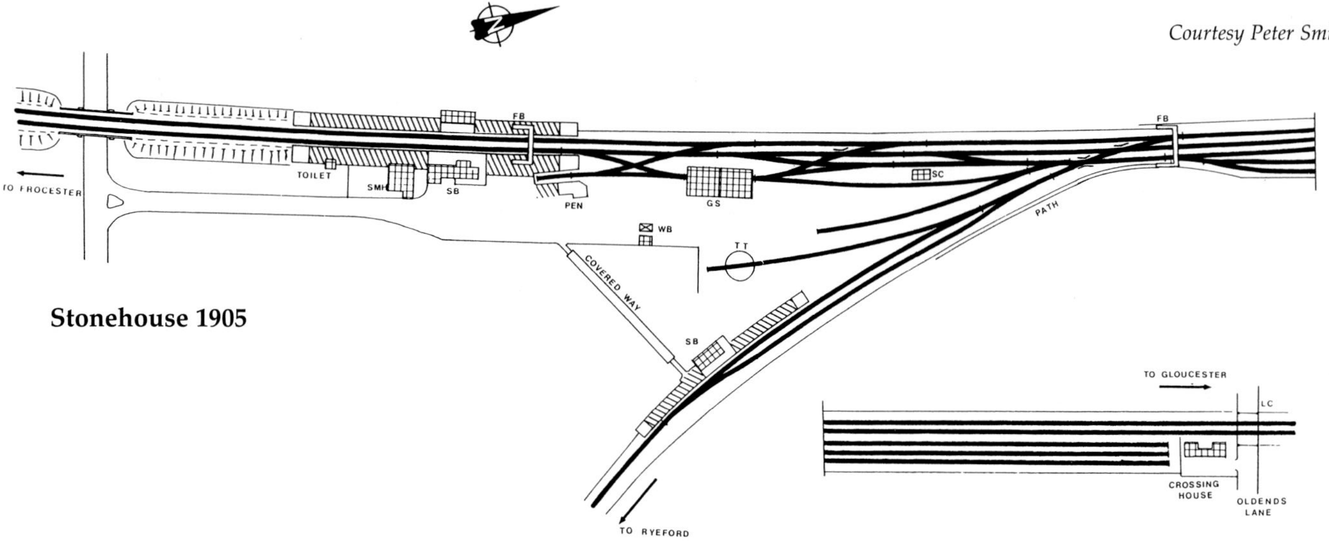

Stonehouse 1905

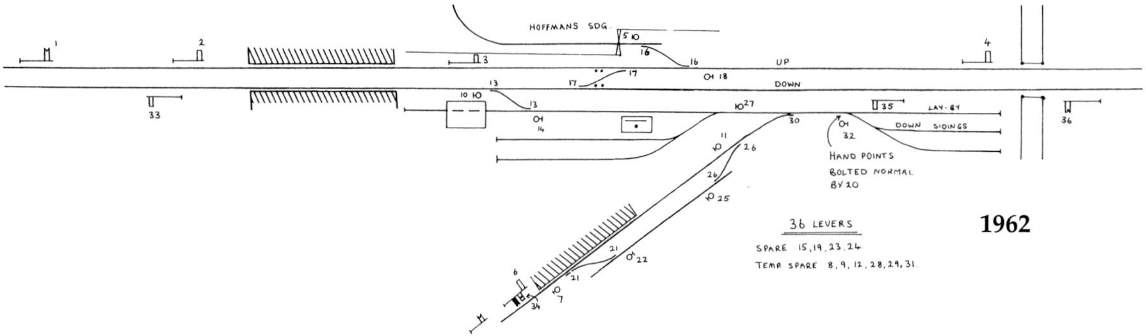

TO STROUD

TO GLOUCESTER

OLDENDS LANE

CROSSING HOUSE

LC

TO RYEFORD

PATH

COVERED WAY

GS

T.T

SB

WB

PEN

FB

SB

SMH

TOILET

N

FB

SC

1962

36

4

35

DOWN SIGNALS

Hand Points
Bolted Normal
8 y 20

36 LEVERS

Spare 15, 19, 23, 24.
Temp Spare 8, 9, 12, 28, 29, 31.

UP

DOWN

HOFFMANS SDG

2

33

1

Chapter Four

Description of the Line

Stonehouse to Nailsworth

Stonehouse, Bristol Road, originally Eastington Road, station was situated 101 miles 59 chains from Derby. The two-road main line station, had its main buildings of Cotswold stone on the down platform and a stone waiting shelter on the up platform. The station, lit by gas, was situated at the southern end of the complex. At the up end of the down platform was the cattle dock, with the stone-built goods shed beyond. The station was equipped with a public weighbridge. Opposite the goods shed were sidings at Hoffman (Gloucester) Limited's engineering works, brought into use on 6th June, 1940, the private siding agreement being terminated on 18th November, 1966. The sharply-curved siding was worked by a 4-wheel diesel-mechanical locomotive built by Muir-Hill Engineering Limited, being their No. 29 of 1927, bought second-hand from AEC, Southall. To the south of the main line station a wool siding, known as 'The Battery' was removed in 1941. Although there was a trailing connection from the branch to the up main line, no through running was possible from the down line without either a reversal or run round. Even the through connection with the up line was taken out on 20th November, 1960 so that reversal was necessary for both entering and leaving the branch. See Chapter Six for method of signalling employed on the Nailsworth and Stroud branches.

The branch passenger platform (101 m. 52 ch.) with timber waiting room, was situated on the single line a short distance down the branch at the south end of a passing or run-round loop. The position of the loop points was indicated by a rare 'fan shape' ground signal as the staff termed it, another example being at the south end of the loop at Nailsworth. A turntable to which there was access from the up line or the loop was removed on 21st January, 1934. The branch platform was connected with the main station by a covered way formed from corrugated iron sheeting and was removed some time between 1956 and 1962. It was not unknown for porters to ride on a four-wheeled barrow loaded with magazines from Arthurs Press, or bacon from Hillier's, down the slope from the branch to the main line platform. A certain amount of skill was required to steer it from a sitting position.

A coal distribution depot was opened on 7th October, 1966 and worked by an 0-4-0 diesel-mechanical locomotive *Dougal*, formerly *Mr Useful*, Drewry Car Co. Ltd No. 2251 and also Vulcan Foundry Ltd D77 of 1947, formerly used at the Bristol Mechanised Coal Company Ltd at Filton Junction Depot and before that by the Barking Jetty Co. Ltd, Creekmouth, Essex.

In 1945 the Stonehouse station staff consisted of a station master, booking clerk and lady clerk, three signalmen, guard, porter/guard, three porters Grade 1, two Grade 2 and a junior, the latter soon dispensed with, a goods checker, horse carter and motor lorry driver. In the BR period the station was supervised by the station master at Stonehouse, Burdett Road. Goods traffic was principally

Station approach on the down side at Stonehouse *c.* 1910.   *Lionel Padin Collection*

Stonehouse station looking towards Gloucester *c.* 1910.   *Lionel Padin Collection*

Station approach on the down side at Stonehouse in January 1965. *A.S. Apperley*

Station master's house and down platform in January 1965. *A.S. Apperley*

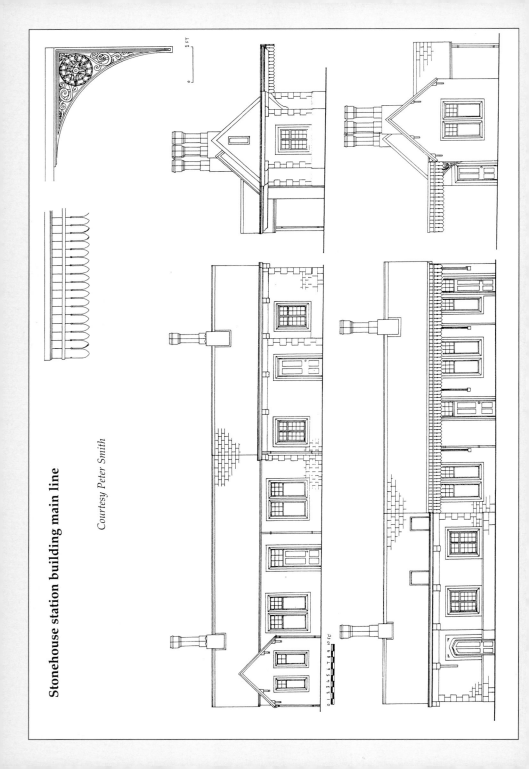

Stonehouse station building main line

Courtesy Peter Smith

A train from Nailsworth to Gloucester regaining the up line at Stonehouse on 11th May, 1961.
Author

The up platform at Stonehouse in January 1965.   *A.S. Apperley*

'9F' class 2-10-0 No. 92217 waits on the down road by Stonehouse goods shed in January 1965.
A.S. Apperley

Diesel-hydraulic type '1' 0-6-0 No. D9502 crosses from the down to the up line at Stonehouse after coming off the branch on 2nd March, 1966. The photograph was taken from the signal box.
D. Payne

Class '3F' 0-6-0 No. 43344 shunts the branch train at Stonehouse. Ex-GWR 2-8-0 No. 3860 passes with an up Western Region train of tank wagons. The covered way between main line and branch platforms is just visible to the left of the signal box. The entrance to Hoffman's sidings is on the right.   *C.S. Cann/Courtesy P.Q. Treloar*

Class '4F' 0-6-0 No. 44264 has come from Gloucester and reverses its train at Stonehouse to reach the Stroud and Nailsworth branch on 30th June, 1965. Note the ex-GWR brake van. Hoffman's siding is on the right.   *W. Potter*

Stonehouse station building branch platform

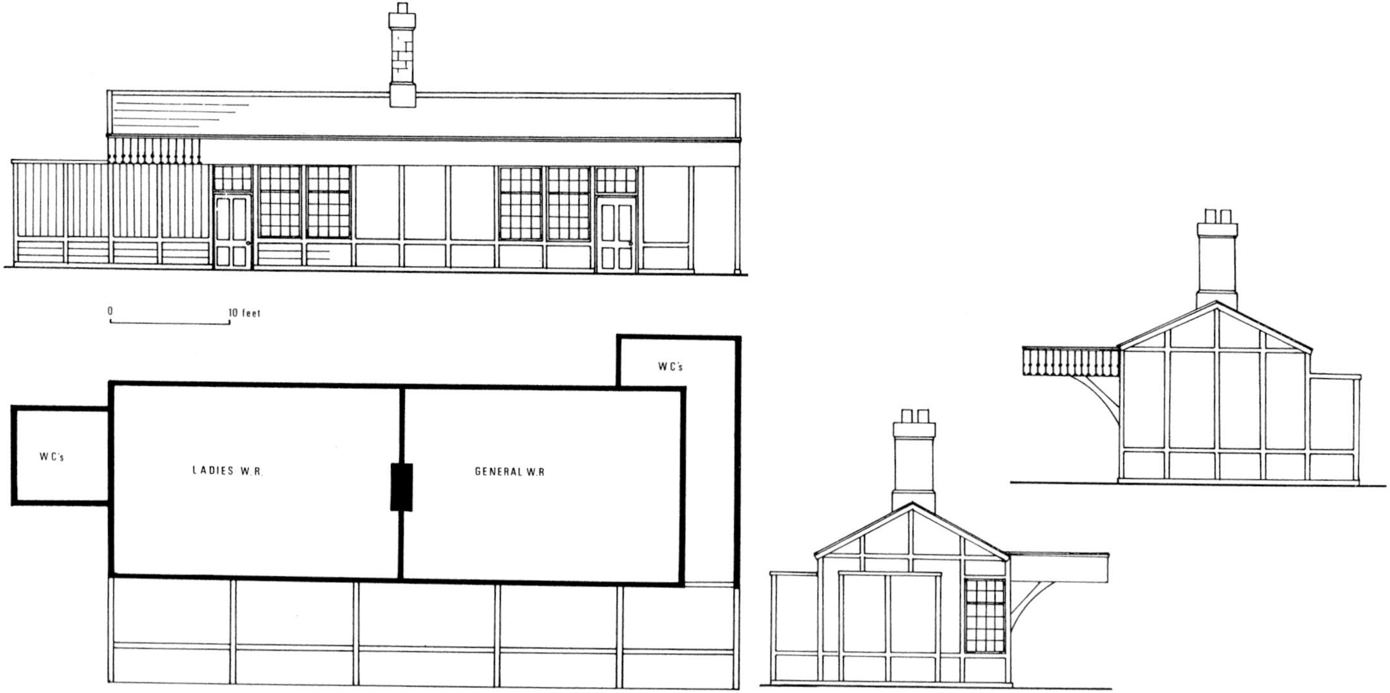

GENERAL W R

LADIES W R

WC's

WC's

0   10 feet

Courtesy Peter Smith

A view from Stonehouse branch platform towards the main line. *Revd W.V. Awdry*

Stonehouse branch platform *c.* 1905. *Author's Collection*

Stonehouse branch platform in 1953, looking towards the main line. *Dr A. Dickens*

View of Stonehouse branch platform from the verandah of departing brake van on the last day of goods service, 1st June, 1966. *D. Payne*

coal, coke, timber, cocoa and powdered milk for Cadbury's factory at Frampton on Severn, potatoes for human consumption, cattle and seed. Wool was dispatched from local mills, hay, and steel swarf from Hoffman's, but there was not much inward traffic for this firm. Sometimes a porter's duty required him to use the large frame, brown station bicycle to go the bank to fetch change for the booking office. The station closed to main line passengers on 4th January, 1965 and to goods, except the private sidings, on 3rd January, 1966.

Beyond the branch platform the line entered a cutting and passed under an occupation footbridge and a cast-iron and masonry bridge carrying the Bristol Road over the line south of Stonehouse. At 102 m. 15 ch. a trailing siding led to Stonehouse Wharf on the Stroudwater Canal. Holding about 11 wagons, it was latterly used as a coal depot until track was lifted on 7th September, 1958. A horsedrawn dray from Stonehouse collected brushes from Vowles' Brushworks and conveyed them to the Wharf for transit by rail. Beyond the siding was Stonehouse Wharf level crossing, commonly called the Ship Inn Crossing. A disabled railwaymen who lived in the gatekeeper's lodge operated the crossing on one turn, the other being covered by staff from Stonehouse. The crossing was manned from 5.00 am till 9.45 pm, or until the last train had passed. A short distance beyond was Vowles' level crossing worked by a man from Stonehouse, with a relief porter on the other turn. It was only manned during the work hours, 8.00 am to 6.00 pm. The trackbed from here to Nailsworth and Stroud has been converted to a cycleway and footpath.

The branch crossed the Stroudwater Canal at 102 m. 37 ch. by a very oblique bridge with a timber land span on the west bank, followed by a steel span of single track width. Piers supporting the span were of unusual construction due to the obliqueness. The bridge was designed by James Ferrabee who founded the Phoenix Ironworks in 1828 at Thrupp Mill in the Stroud Valley. The contractors encountered difficulty with the subsidence of the supporting piers. A few months before closure, the timber span was set alight and the track had to be shored up on 'military trestles' - these being steel plates top and bottom joined by a steel upright. In due course this temporary shoring was replaced by concrete. Because of the obliqueness, the railway ran close beside the canal for a distance, this requiring a longish brick retaining wall east of the bridge. Then follows a blue brick bridge carrying the line over the River Frome. West of Ryeford the line was carried on an embankment.

On 27th March, 1965 transformers were brought for installation at an electricity sub-station west of the overbridge at Ryeford. The lowloader bringing them would have grounded on the humped-back canal bridge, so they were brought by road to Vowles' Crossing, off-loaded on to rail wagons and hauled by 0-6-0 No. 44123 to a specially built concrete pad where they were lifted off by a private crane. The track itself was strengthened by extra sleepers being laid. At this spot a trailing siding led to Marling & Evans' Mill, originally Stanley Mills. Major General C.S. Hutchinson inspected the new siding on 9th October, 1890. It was worked from a three-lever dwarf ground frame released by an interlocking lever in Ryeford signal box. The siding was lifted on 7th July, 1930. Stanley Marling was a daily passenger between Dudbridge and Ryeford on his way from Stanley Park to his mills and back. His evening train from

Bridge No. 2, view towards Stonehouse.   *Revd W.V. Awdry*

Bridge No. 3, carrying the Bristol Road.   *Revd W.V. Awdry*

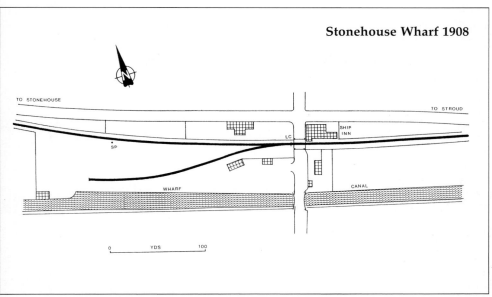

Plan of Stonehouse Wharf 1908. *Courtesy Peter Smith*

Stonehouse Wharf on the Stroudwater Canal *c.* 1900. Railway wagons can be seen on the left.
Author's Collection

Plan of Stonehouse Wharf Crossing House

Courtesy Peter Smith

0 2 4 6 8 10 ft

BR Standard class '2MT' 2-6-0 No. 78004 passes over the Ship Inn crossing with an up goods, 12th May, 1965.   *W. Potter*

Opening the gates at Brushworks crossing, a view from the cab of diesel-hydraulic type '1' 0-6-0 No. D9502 on 2nd March, 1966.   *D. Payne*

Bridge No. 4 over the Stroudwater Canal, looking towards Ryeford. Charred timber can be seen
on the left.   *Revd W.V. Awdry*

Bridge No. 4. Concrete replacement can be seen on the left.   *Author*

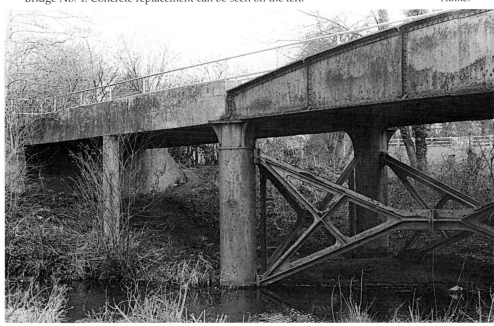

BR Standard class '2MT' 2-6-0 No. 78004 crosses Stroudwater Canal with a train for Dudbridge, 21st May, 1965. Temporary supports for the charred timber can be seen on the left.

B.J. Ashworth

A special train with a transformer for Ryeford Midlands Electricity sub-station on 29th March, 1965.   *D. Payne*

Messrs Hathway wagon No. 1. Painted a lead colour with white lettering shaded black, it was built by the Gloucester Railway Carriage & Wagon Co. in February 1907.   *P.J. Smith Collection*

Ryeford to Dudbridge was scheduled to leave at 5.39 pm and if he had to delay his departure from the mill for a few minutes, he used to send a messenger with the request for the train to be held.

Ryeford station, (102 m. 63 ch.) had a single, unusually wide platform on the south side of the line, with offices and a stone-built station master's house with a quarter-acre garden. The porch was supported by pillars with carved capitals. A goods shed and cattle food store on concrete stilts to keep vermin away were beyond, while to the north was a siding dealing with large blocks of Bath stone until *circa* 1910. Also to the north were sidings to Ryeford Mills dealing in both wood and corn, latterly timber arriving by road and going away by rail. A weighbridge was sited in the station yard. The goods shed line ceased to be a loop on 7th April, 1933. The signal box with a 12-lever frame, two levers being spare, opened in November 1885 in preparation for the increased traffic when the Stroud branch was opened. The box closed on 7th September, 1958 and was replaced by two ground frames. This was a block post but not a staff station and no staffs were issued. The box was open only as required for freight trains stopping at the station for traffic purposes and the signals also used for the protection of the crossing when traction engines, or heavy loads of timber, were passing over it. In the 1920s it was not unusual for the passenger platform to the three deep with villagers from Leonard Stanley and Kings Stanley holding a 3*d.* return to Stroud.

Staff consisted of a station master, two porters and a signalman in the early days, but towards closure was whittled down to two Grade 1 porter-signalmen, one on each turn carrying out all duties. This was quite an undertaking for there was a Silcocks' depot from which farmers collected cattle cake, or sometimes it was delivered by railway lorry, in both instances the porter-signalman being responsible for checking it in and out, while timber sent from the mill had to be measured up as this commodity was subject to different rates. Smoke canisters were burnt in the cattle feed shed periodically to prevent moths breeding in the hessian sacks. When the branch closed, the feed store was removed by BR for use elsewhere.

Quite a large culvert passed under the station house and the line in the vicinity of the station was prone to flooding. Following heavy rain, the first engine to Stroud on 31st December, 1901 had its fire doused by flood water. About 1931 due to two feet of water covering the track, a goods train was stopped by the signalman at Dudbridge Sidings and the driver warned of the flood, but he decided to proceed. The signalman listened and eventually the noise of the train died away . . . he thought the train must be stuck in the flood . . . then he heard the engine climbing the gradient the other side and knew it had got through safely. In 1947 flooding closed the line for a day. *Circa* 1964 the roof of the station house was leaking and to save expense of re-roofing, hessian and tar were applied. The station closed to passengers on 16th June, 1947 and to goods on 1st June, 1964. About 1957 a traction engine was taken from Ryeford to Yorkshire. It was one of the last times the loading bay was used and one of the last traction engines to be sent by rail. Following closure of the branch, Ryeford station was demolished, though the booking office equipment and panelling is preserved by the Dean Forest Railway Society at Norchard.

Ryeford station 1920

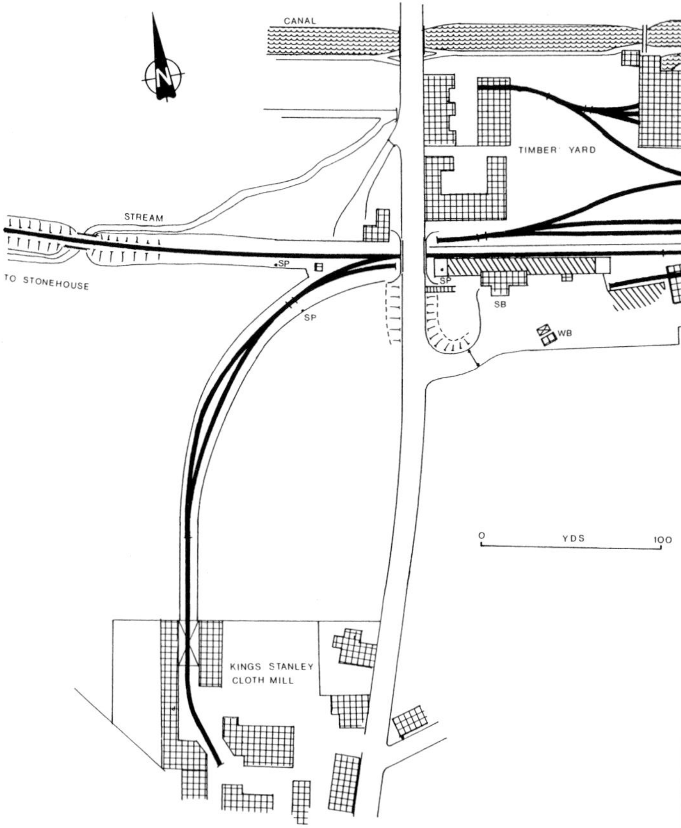

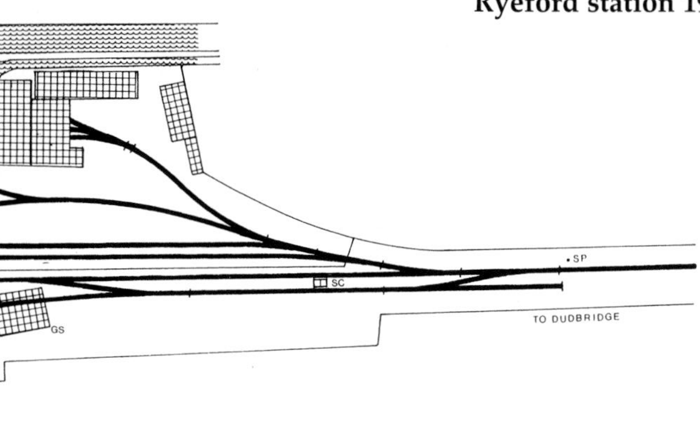

Ryeford c. 1925, looking towards Dudbridge. The signal box can be seen beyond the goods shed.
P.J. Smith Collection

TO DUDBRIDGE

SC

GS

WB

SB

SP

TIMBER YARD

CANAL

STREAM

TO STONEHOUSE

SP

SP

KINGS STANLEY CLOTH MILL

N

YDS   0   100

Courtesy Peter Smith

Road frontage of Ryeford station, *c.* 1905. Notice the attractive portico on the left and also the flower beds and creepers. *Author's Collection*

Ryeford *c.* 1905. Marling & Evans' siding curves to the left beyond the bridge and also the rising gradient can be seen. The station master is on the platform dressed in a long coat. *Author's Collection*

Above: A Stonehouse to Stroud and Nailsworth goods passing through Ryeford. Notice Silcocks' feedstuffs store, the signal box (closed 7th September, 1958) and timber mill on the left.   *Author*

Right: Ryeford station house with portico entrance. *Revd W.V. Awdry*

Ryeford goods shed and feedstuffs store, view looking towards Stonehouse. *Revd W.V. Awdry*

The goods office, Ryeford, 1963. *A.S. Apperley*

The very low bridge over the River Frome east of Ryeford, view south.   *Author*

Lane's siding, 1920.   *Courtesy Peter Smith*

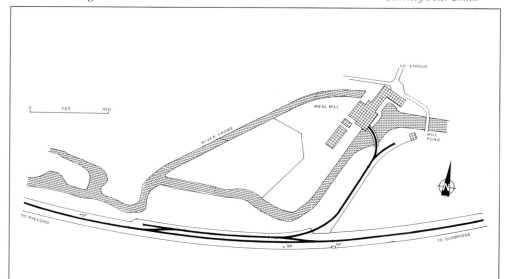

Lane's siding 1920

East of Ryeford the line was on a low embankment with drainage ditches either side. At 103 m. 16 ch. a steel girder bridge, of single track width, crosses the River Frome and is remarkable for the fact that the clearance between normal water level and the underside of the girders is only about 3½ feet. Beyond the bridge, where the line was level with the fields, flooding was experienced as ground level was not much above the normal level of the Frome. At 103 m. 41 ch. was Lane's Siding ground frame. From this siding, holding about 30 wagons, a private line crossed Ebley Meadows - privately owned land with grazing rights to commoners, and led to A.W. Smith & Sons' mill. Until traffic ceased *circa* 1937, two wagons of cattle feed arrived every other day and each was drawn by a shire horse from the siding to the mill. The feed in hessian sacks was lifted out of the wagons by hoist operated by a water wheel. The private siding agreement terminated on 30th June, 1942 and subsequently the line was sold for scrap to help the war effort. Until 12th June, 1933 the siding giving access to Lane's siding was a loop, the ground frame at 103 m. 31 ch. being closed on this date, and removed sometime after 1951. During World War II Lane's siding was used for bringing supplies to United States' troops, vans arriving with sugar, boots, clothing and so on, the army collecting them in road vehicles. At one period the siding was filled with wagons of gas coal in order to ease crowded conditions in Gloucester yard. The wagons sometimes stayed there for months and after being stationary for so long, the grease in the axle boxes became so solid that they were hard to shift. From Lane's siding the line climbed at 1 in 77 on an embankment.

Immediately before Dudbridge Sidings signal box, 103 m. 71 ch., was a brick-arch occupation bridge in blue bricks. West of the box was a stop signal which it operated, and two distant signals worked from the Junction box. The nameboard at Dudbridge, 104 m. 6 ch., read 'Dudbridge Junction for Stroud & Nailsworth'. Originally only having a platform on the north side of the line, this was lengthened and a new up platform constructed immediately prior to the opening of the Stroud branch. On the platform was the body of a six-wheel passenger full brake, first used as a porters' room and latterly a permanent way mess hut. It had a fireplace and on a wet day it was the practice of a coal merchant to dry out both his sacks and his clothes in front of it. BR eventually built a permanent way cabin at the up end of the yard only a few years before closure. Also on the platform was a four-wheel box van body used for storing parcels which could not be delivered immediately. The lamp room in the abutment of the overbridge east of the station was rendered superfluous after closure of the box and the removal of signals in 1957 and was utilised then as a store. The station was lit by gas. The rails at Dudbridge occasionally became flooded and the station house was damp. The permanent way department received complaints of a rail joint outside the house causing vibration. Little could be done because of the damp - chippings placed under the sleeper by permanent way men only giving support for a couple of days.

Dudbridge, the most important intermediate station on the branch, had double line block working over the just over a quarter of a mile between the two signal boxes.

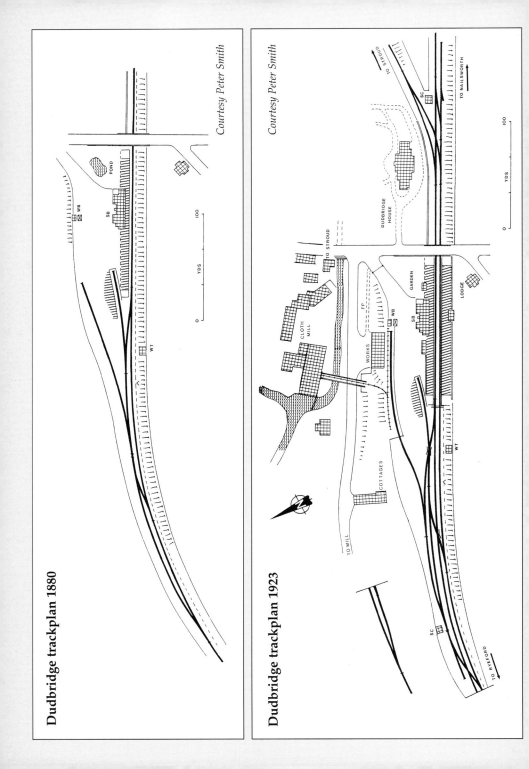

Dudbridge trackplan 1880

Courtesy Peter Smith

Dudbridge trackplan 1923

Courtesy Peter Smith

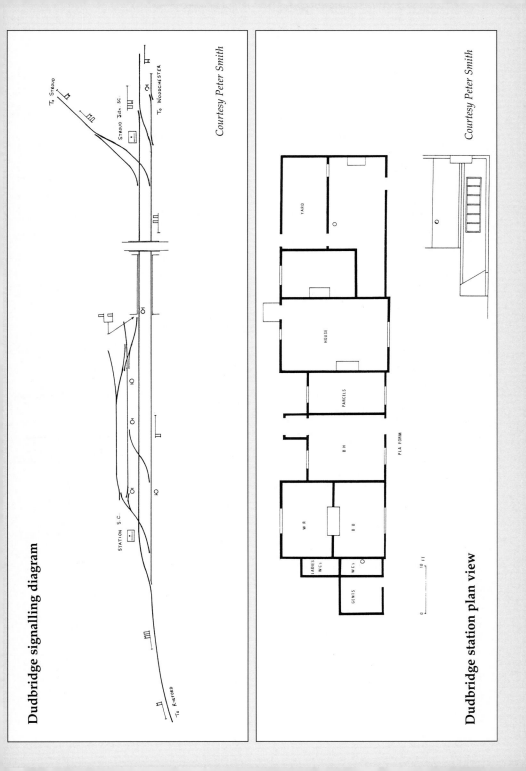

Dudbridge signalling diagram

Courtesy Peter Smith

Dudbridge station plan view

Courtesy Peter Smith

Dudbridge station buildings

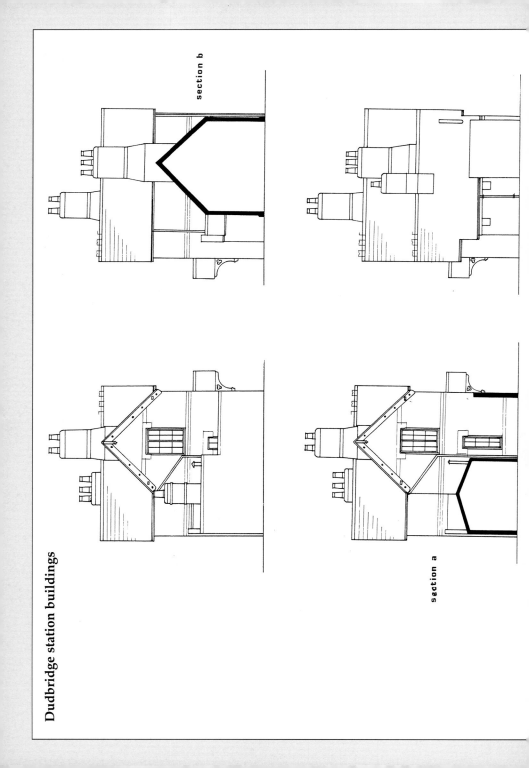

section b

section a

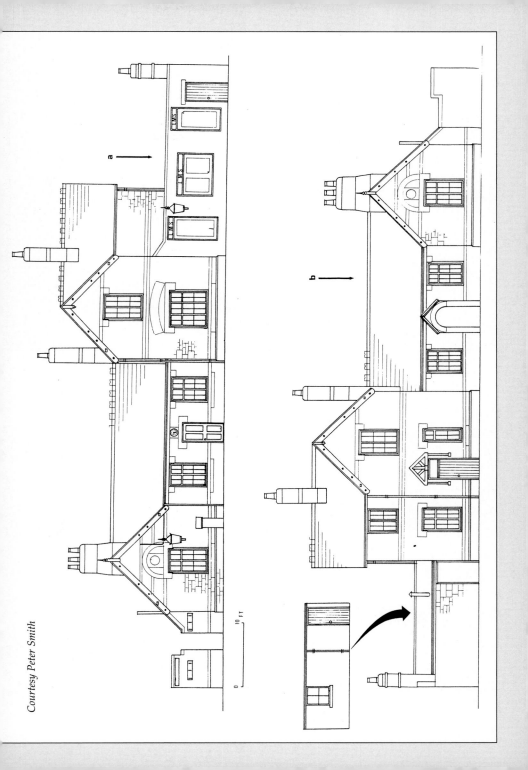

Courtesy Peter Smith

An aerial view of Dudbridge in 1926 looking north. The goods yard is at the foot of the picture immediately above the line of trees. Notice the narrow gauge railway entering Kimmins' Mill at the third storey.

Miss E. Halliday Collection

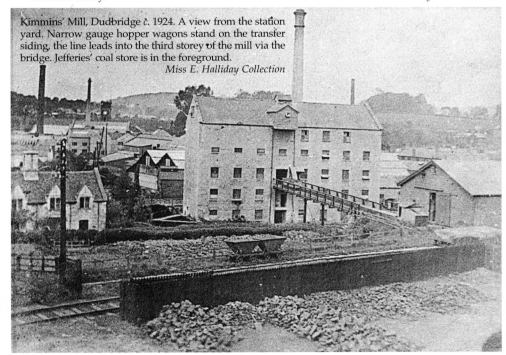

Kimmins' Mill, Dudbridge c. 1924. A view from the station yard. Narrow gauge hopper wagons stand on the transfer siding, the line leads into the third storey of the mill via the bridge. Jefferies' coal store is in the foreground.

Miss E. Halliday Collection

Dudbridge Junction on 31st May, 1956. Note the scythe outside the permanent way mess hut.
Author

Dudbridge station buildings from the approach in 1965. Notice the coal merchant's store on the right.   *S.N. Adam*

The weighbridge and office, Dudbridge, September 1961.   *K. Ofield*

The Sectional Appendix to the Working Timetable, October 1960, stated that a wheel stop was provided at the Stonehouse end of the up sidings and this was required to be kept across the line and padlocked in position except when movement was taking place between the sidings and the single line at that end of the yard. This precaution was necessary because of the falling gradient of 1 in 77 towards Ryeford. The wheel stop key was kept in the station master's office.

One of the strange features of Dudbridge was that there was no goods shed - unusual for a layout of its size. The station had a public weighbridge, but neither horse dray nor motor lorry, parcel delivery being by LMS bicycle with a basket on the front, or else by handcart. For delivery of larger items with which Dudbridge's own 'transport' could not cope, the lorry from Stroud was used. Besides a coal road and cattle dock, there was a transfer siding with a tramway to the adjacent Kimmins' flour mill, narrow gauge trucks being pushed by hand across a steel bridge to the third storey. Although originally water-powered, a gas engine was installed in the factory workshop and small coal came by rail to generate the gas. The tramway had two types of wagon: hoppers for coal and flat trucks for sacks of wheat which came from Russia and Canada. Traffic ceased in 1931 when it was no longer a flour mill. The station dealt with considerable traffic: gas engines made by Dudbridge Iron Works were loaded on rail wagons by block and tackle; traffic was received from the Stroud Metal Company, Copeland Chatterson Printing Company, James & Owen Printing Works, Apperley Curtis at Dudbridge MIlls which manufactured West of England cloth, a dye works, G. Wedel & Son an offal factory making sausage skins and violin strings, a pattern maker for engineering firms. Daniels Engineering Works sent 2½ cwt boxes from Lightmill which were heavy for lady porters to lift.

During World War II the Royal Navy took over the station yard and stored full barrels of oil for smoke screen use and were periodically sent to a naval base in 40 to 50 wagons at a time. Cables and jeeps were also stored at Dudbridge. Since 1939 traffic was mainly inwards - domestic coal, raw materials for farms and steel works, coke and pig iron, outwards traffic being scarce apart from swarf from steel works destined for Guest, Keen & Baldwin at Port Talbot. It was brought by lorry which backed against a railway wagon for transfer. There were outwards parcels of plastics from Erinoid Limited. Cattle and sheep arrived for the abattoir at Ebley, often in a truck on the rear of a passenger train drawn by an 0-6-0. Cattle were driven by road from the station to Ebley. A lady porter had to count them as they left the yard, but they often went so fast on being released from the pen that she had difficulty. This traffic ceased *circa* 1946, the cattle dock not being used after this date. Pigs went to Smith Rogers for bacon. An occasional horse box was dispatched from Dudbridge. In the 1930s Sir Percival Marling had a truck of coal delivered to Dudbridge and sent a dray pulled by shire horses to take it up to Stanley Park. In 1954 a total of 38,000 tons of minerals and goods were conveyed to and from Dudbridge, Woodchester and Nailsworth stations.

When giving performances in Victory Park, Cainscross, both Chipperfield's and Bertram Mills' circuses came by train. The latter arrived in 1951 in three

Bertram Mills' Circus train at Dudbridge, 1951.   *K. Ofield*

Bertram Mills' elephant in the circus train at Dudbridge, 1951.   *K. Ofield*

BRITISH RAILWAYS : LONDON MIDLAND OPERATING AREA. **E.R.O.** 24169

LONDON MIDLAND AND SCOTTISH RAILWAY COMPANY

F. SPARKES,
District Operating Manager Supt.,

Telephone: Gloucester 5171. Ext..............
Telegrams. "Operating, L M S Gloucester."

YOUR REFERENCE

OUR REFERENCE

G.Pad.39.

Supt's.
DISTRICT OPERATING MANAGER'S OFFICE,
GLOUCESTER,

14th September, 19 51.

Mr.Ofield,
Station Master,
DUDBRIDGE.

PERSONAL.

Dear Ofield,

Bertram Mills Circus Tour - 1951.

After having seen you a few days ago, I was in no doubt at all that you would see to it that the movement of the three Circus trains from your station would be carried out efficiently.

My confidence in you has been well confirmed and I should like to take this opportunity of specially thanking you and your staff for what I know to be a most creditable performance.

Your interest and cooperation with my District Inspector Moss produced results which gave every satisfaction to the Circus Officials.

Please convey to all concerned my appreciation of such a splendid effort.

Yours sincerely,

[signature]

Letter of thanks with regard to the circus, sent to station master Ken Ofield.

Dudbridge staff *circa* 1924. The booking clerk and station master are not in the picture.

Miss E. Halliday Collection

Dudbridge station delivery bicycle *circa* 1945; the sister of the station master is posed on it. Coal pens can be seen in the background.

K. Ofield

trains, all double-headed by class '4' 0-6-0s. Ken Ofield, station master at the time, worked 36 hours without a break when the circus was there. The circus stipulated that vans should be marshalled in a certain order. Not all circus vehicles could be stored at Dudbridge - some were sent to Stroud, Nailsworth, Woodchester, Ryeford and others back to Stonehouse. Tilley lamps were specially supplied so that loading and unloading could be carried out at night.

A water tank on the embankment west of the up platform was gravity fed from a spring on the hill and was also supplied by mains water at 2s. 6d. per 1,000 gallons. There was a water column at the end of the up platform. Once when an engine on the main line at Stonehouse ran low on water and the driver was afraid his fusible plug would melt, he conveyed his anxiety to the signalman who asked him if he knew the road to Dudbridge. On being given a reply in the affirmative, he went to Dudbridge to replenish his tank.

Mr Denley, station master in the 1930s was well-known for keeping chickens, ducks, goats and rabbits in hutches round the perimeter of the station yard, almost converting it into a farm. The staff in 1947 consisted of a station master, two porters and four signalmen/women. The porter cleaned the floor of the waiting room daily, worked the weighbridge and issued tickets for it, issued and collected tickets from passengers and fetched cheques from local factories. Ken Ofield was appointed station master in 1940, eventually taking over all stations on the branch including Stonehouse, Bristol Road. He lived in the station house until it was demolished in the 1970s when plans were produced for building a by-pass along the formation. In LMS days cash was sent to be banked at Lloyds, Nailsworth, but in BR times it was sent to Bristol. The wages cash came from Gloucester by passenger train, the guard signing for it at Gloucester and the station master signing at Dudbridge. After the cessation of the passenger service the Nailsworth station master brought it by bus to Dudbridge in a Gladstone bag, but when he was withdrawn, Ofield went to Nailsworth by bus to collect wages from the bank, the railway reimbursing him if he attached tickets to an expenses sheet. The safe key at Dudbridge was kept in the Edmondson ticket dating press. Dudbridge station was used by villagers from Kings Stanley and Selsley, 20 to 30 passengers using the station daily in the 1940s including about six season ticket holders, while up to 100 passengers travelled to Gloucester on a Saturday afternoon. Like the rest of the branch passenger traffic ceased on 16th June, 1947 and the station closed to goods on 1st June, 1966.

Beyond Dudbridge Junction box, 104 m. 14 ch., the line reverted to single and a facing siding, opened on 10th March, 1901 on the west side of the line at 104 m. 52 ch. gave access to J.C. Kimmins & Company's brickworks, but was disused by 1922. it was worked only by an up train, admission being by single lever ground frame locked by the train staff. At 105 m. 10 ch. on the east side of the line was the trailing Matthew Grist's Mill siding. Originally Rooksmoor siding, it was Grist's siding in the Railway Clearing House list of January 1917. Feathers arrived for re-cycling, rags came by rail as did coke for the boiler, Matthew Grist having his own wagon with his name on it. Men became smothered when loading the half-hundredweight bales into a van, 40 such bales being tightly packed in. Often three to four railway vans were filled daily. The private siding agreement terminated on 16th May, 1964.

Ken Ofield, station master, Dudbridge, 1941.   *K. Ofield Collection*

Class '3F' 0-6-0 No. 43373 shunting at Dudbridge on 8th July, 1955. Notice the water column at the far end of the up platform. *Hugh Ballantyne*

Diesel-hydraulic type '1' 0-6-0 No. D9500 is seen at Dudbridge with empty coal wagons from Nailsworth on 27th May, 1966. *W. Potter*

Dudbridge Junction on 7th May, 1955. The bracket signal had replaced an earlier single post signal (*see page 120*).   *Author*

Dudbridge Junction on 3rd March, 1966 after simplification of the track and removal of the signal box.   *Revd W.V. Awdry*

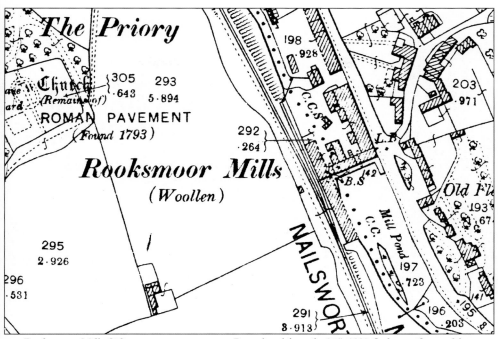

Rooksmoor Mills Siding.

Reproduced from the 25", 1902 Ordnance Survey Map

Platelayers' hut at Rooksmoor siding.

Revd W.V. Awdry

Matthew Grist wagon No. 2 painted lead grey with white letters shaded black. Built by the Gloucester Railway Carriage & Wagon Co.   *P.J. Smith Collection*

Messrs Harris wagon No. 21. Painted black with white lettering it was built by Gloucester Railway Carriage & Wagon Co. in December 1893.   *P.J. Smith Collection*

A brick overbridge with vaulting carries Selsley Road across the line. A single-track bridge crosses a stream known as the Avon, the oblique bridge having a wooden deck. Today the track formation is obliterated for about 100 yds north of Woodchester by road improvements. Bird's, or Arthurs Press, level crossing north of Woodchester had a gatekeeper's house, a lengthman living there and his wife looking after the crossing.

Woodchester, 105 m. 49 ch., had a single platform on the east side of the line, the station building being of timber and unusually creosoted and not painted. The ladies' waiting room had an open fire and so was used by all in winter regardless of gender. At one time the station enjoyed heavy holiday traffic in summer when tourists visited Amberley, the 'Enderley' of *John Halifax, Gentleman*, while Dunkirk Mills were supposedly the mills of John Halifax. Latterly, passenger traffic was light apart from a few people on the first train. One regular commuter was S.S. Marling who was brought in by his chauffeur to catch the train to his cloth mill at Ryeford. The porter who carried his attaché case from car to train was tipped sixpence. At one time Woodchester was one of the busiest goods stations on the MR in Gloucestershire and for three consecutive years won a shield given to the station in the Gloucester District which had the greatest amount of parcels traffic. The goods yard with its three sidings and private siding to Henry Workman's timber mill was on the far side of the level crossing. The General Appendix to the Working Timetables dated 1st January, 1931 ruled:

> The connection between the second and third sidings from the mainline at the Nailsworth end of Woodchester goods yard is worked by guards and shunters from a stage, and controlled by a key, which is kept in the lever frame at the stage.
> Before Messrs Workman's steam travelling crane is allowed to foul the third siding from the main line in Woodchester goods yard, Messrs Workman's servants must obtain possession of the key in order to prevent LMS engines from entering the siding, and as soon as the crane has returned into Messrs Workman's yard, the key must be at once replaced in the lever frame. In the event of a LMS train requiring to enter the third siding from the main line in Woodchester goods yard during the time Messrs Workman's servants have possession of the key, Messrs Workman's servants must be requested to place the crane clear of Woodchester goods yard sidings, and return the key to the lever frame.

The private siding agreement terminated on 11th February, 1964. The steam crane was low geared and crossed the A46 slowly to the great irritation of car drivers. The A46 had to be protected by a man either side of the crossing. The crane burnt offcuts of wood. Most of the timber arrived by road, was sawn up and dispatched by rail. The firm made oak keys to secure rails in chairs. Workers at the sawmill fitted handles into railwaymen's tools free of charge. Arthurs Press printed periodicals and posters for cinemas. The bulk of paper for the firm arrived by rail, and magazines were dispatched in a coaching stock van. Carr Tanning had sheep skins delivered by rail, they were turned into leather which was sent away by rail. Incubators were made at Woodchester and forwarded by rail. Timber for making the incubators was kept in wagons at Stonehouse and six or seven wagons were sent up each day as room could be made for them. During World War II there was a NAAFI depot at Woodchester

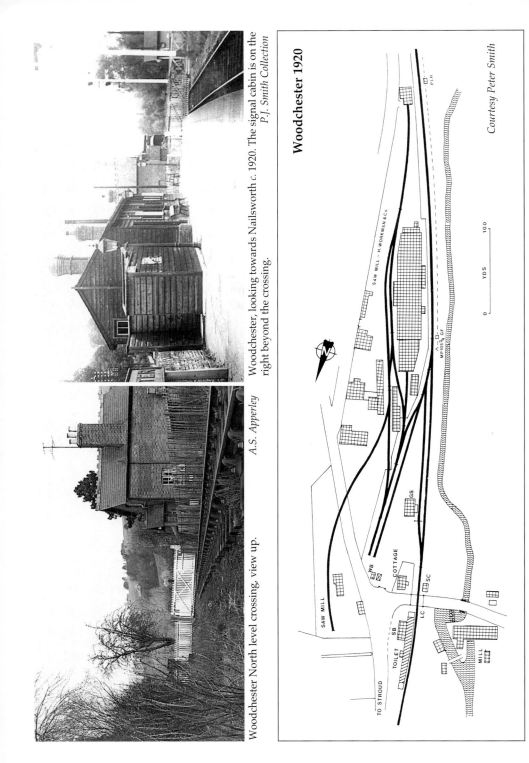

Woodchester North level crossing, view up.

A.S. Apperley

Woodchester, looking towards Nailsworth *c*. 1920. The signal cabin is on the right beyond the crossing.

P.J. Smith Collection

Woodchester 1920

Courtesy Peter Smith

0   YDS   100

SAW MILL — H. WORKMAN & Co

TO STROUD

SAW MILL

TOILET

SB

WB

COTTAGE

SC

LC

MILL

GS

MP105¼ GF

PLH

Woodchester station *c.* 1935 with the telegraph lineman up his ladder. *P. Strong Collection*

Woodchester in 1953. The station master's, later porter's house can be seen in the background.
Dr A. Dickens

Henry Workman's steam crane used for lifting and shunting at Woodchester. This view is taken from the 1907 *Illustrated Guide to Stroud & Its Neighbourhood.*　　*Courtesy S. Gardiner*

The timber-built goods shed at Woodchester.　　*Revd W.V. Awdry*

and goods for it came by train both in and out. The United States army was stationed at Woodchester and their supplies arrived by rail. Stroud Piano Company used road more than rail because of breakages. A hair pin factory provided traffic and J. Long, coal merchant, received loaded mineral wagons. Woodchester had a weighbridge, but no cattle pen. The station closed to goods on 1st June, 1964.

At one time the staff consisted of a station master, two porters who worked in the station and goods yard, a junior porter and three clerks in the office for invoicing. The porter on late shift had to work until the last train came up the branch, unless he was informed that there were no passengers on it. During World War II the last train was sometimes as much as three hours late because the branch connection had to be held for the main line train. The porter on the late turn was also responsible for the gas lamps. Officially these were supposed to be turned off individually, but to save time all lights were doused by pushing down a lever on the right-hand side of the main door. Another duty of the porter was to open the crossing gates. He received 'Train on Line' from Dudbridge Junction, but no warning of approaching up trains because there was no signal box at Nailsworth. The signals were not always used at Woodchester, sometimes a train was just beckoned on by hand to save walking to the frame after the porter had opened the gates. There was a store in the ground frame cabin which doubled as a mess room. It was removed in 1959 to become a garden shed and is still extant. At night the crossing gates were padlocked and a carriage key used to lock the wicket gates to the platform. The driver of the horse dray was A. Ashinford, the LMS horse being stabled in the round tower, now a house, but originally a bleaching tower, then a teasel tower, before becoming the MR stable. Walter Matthews, of the Forge, Woodchester, shod the railway horses and a man was sent from Gloucester when the dray required repair.

A brick overbridge similar to that at Selsley Road, carried the A46 over the branch and was paralleled *circa* 1964 by a new, wider bridge of concrete. The old bridge is now part of a lay-by. The base of Woodchester up distant and the base of its signal ladder can still be seen south of the overbridges.

Newman Hender's siding trailed in from the west side of the line at 106 m. 33 ch. Opened on 18th January, 1920 and coming under the control of Woodchester, it had a sharp curve sometimes derailing the engine or wagons and causing the Gloucester breakdown gang to come out with a steam crane. The original siding on the east side of the line at 106 m. 36 ch., put in under a private siding agreement of 11th September, 1869, was taken out of use on 18th January, 1920.

Newman Hender's was an engineering firm making pumps, valves, etc. and *circa* 1896 the first Suction Gas Plant in England was introduced at these works supplying gas to a Dudbridge gas engine of about 90 hp. The firm made munitions during World War I - ordnance fuses, shell primers and many larger engineering products calling for close limits of tolerance, over 1,000 workpeople being employed. During World War II it again worked on armaments, among other thousands of munitions parts they produced over 40 million fuses and primers. The firm received iron ingots, coal and coke by rail and sand for

The tower (originally used for bleaching, then for drying teasels) used as the MR stables at Woodchester.   *Author*

Bridge No. 17 carrying the A46 Bath Road over the line south of Woodchester, original span.
Revd W.V. Awdry

Bath Road bridge, bridge No. 17, showing the new span with the original bridge beyond.
A.S. Apperley

Above: BR Standard class '2MT' 2-6-0 No. 78006 at Newman Hender's siding on 16th August, 1965. The ground frame can be seen on the left. *D. Payne*

Right: A mineral wagon having run through catch points at Newman Hender's siding on 16th August, 1965. *D. Payne*

casting. In 1966 it received 30 tons of pig iron and 10 tons of coke weekly and, shortly before closure of the branch was announced, the firm completed the erection of a covered way from the siding to the foundry. An electro-magnetic crane came into use for unloading pig iron just before the trains stopped running.

The Sectional Appendix to the Working Timetable for 1937 laid down rules for working the siding situated where the main line was on a gradient of 1 in 421 falling towards Dudbridge. In order that the brake van could prevent runaways, only down trains were permitted to shunt the siding. Vehicles could not be placed in or removed from the siding until the guard or shunter had obtained permission from the firm's foreman for this to be done. Wagons in the shed were coupled together and made ready for drawing out by the firm's staff, LMS employees not being allowed to enter the shed. LMS staff working the siding were ordered to do so, if possible, from the main line. It was the usual practice for coke wagons for Newman Hender's to be placed near the engine, though a driver liked to have four wagons in front to make sure that the engine was not derailed on the curve. The empties were pulled out and gently backed on to the brake van. It could be precarious when they went back as sometimes the brake failed to hold and the rake rolled down the gradient. On at least one occasion about three wagons and a brake van ran away through the gates to Woodchester, the porter from that station chasing after them and bringing them to a halt near Grist's siding. After removal of the empties from Newman Hender's siding, full wagons were put in.

A timber bridge over the line by Newman Hender's gave a short cut for workers to and from the Box district, the bridge deteriorated with age and was reconstructed in concrete in 1953. Only one abutment needed renewing. A trailing siding to Grove Saw Mill closed just prior to World War I. Dunkirk siding trailed on the west side of the line at 106 m. 64 ch. Deleted in the Railway Clearing House list of September 1946, it was lifted 14 months later. Dunkirk Mills were Walker's stick mills, producing wooden handles and walking sticks, not providing much rail traffic.

Nailsworth station was a single platform on the east side of the line at 107 m. 10 ch. The Cotswold stone building with its fine architecture befitting the principal SNR station and containing the company's offices, still stands at the end of a long carriage drive. In front of the door a little arcade is carried on leafy capitals as at Ryeford. There is a similarity between these carvings and that by Joshua Wall in Stroud Parish Church finished a year before the line opened. The slated roof surmounted by red decorative ridge tiles has been tarred to make it weatherproof. A porters' room built of brick was at the end of the platform. the station was lit by oil. The station's initial paintwork must have been of poor quality as on 16th March, 1869, just over two years after opening, E. Niblett's tender was accepted for cleaning, papering and painting the buildings for £14 10s. 0d.

Footwarmers were still used on branch trains in the 1930s. At Nailsworth they were put in a boiler in the evening and it was damped down. Next morning a porter lifted them out with a hooked stick and placed them in each compartment occupied by adults, but not children. He also took boiling water to thaw the points. The Post Office sent mail by train, the postman going to the

Above: The timber-built Newman Hender's bridge *circa* 1910, view up the line.

Lionel Padin Collection

Right: Reconstruction of the overbridge near Newman Hender's *circa* 1953, a concrete beam being laid in place by a steam crane.

R. Buckley Collection

Bridge No. 18 and platelayers' hut at Newman Hender's. The new bridge uses the old abutment on the left-hand side. *A.S. Apperley*

Grove saw mill siding. *Reproduced from the 25", 1885 Ordnance Survey Map*

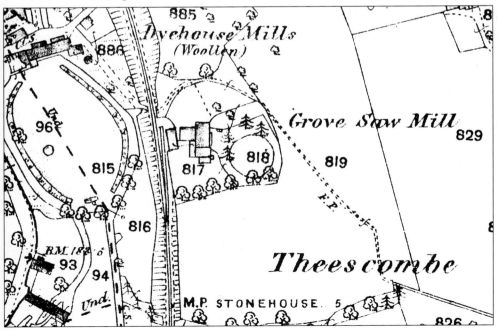

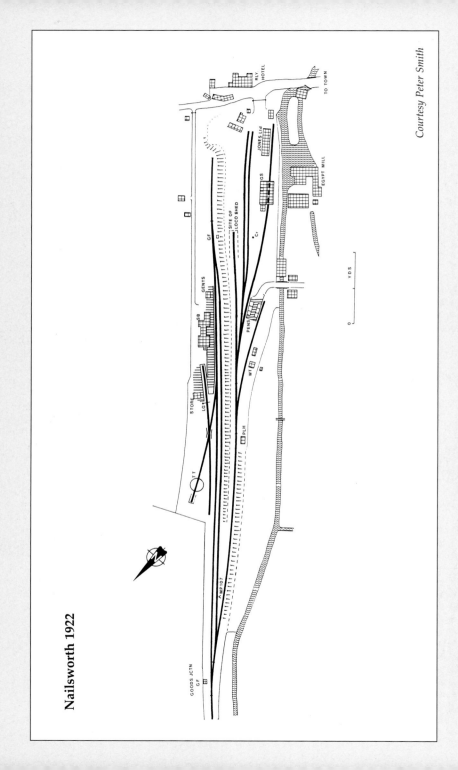

Nailsworth 1922

Courtesy Peter Smith

station with a handcart to meet trains. Following a court session at Nailsworth, prisoners for Gloucester gaol could be seen proceeding to the station handcuffed to a policeman.

The passenger station was situated at a higher level than the goods yard as the original intention was that the railway would be extended southwards. Access to the yard, colloquially known as 'down the hole' was by facing point protected by lock and key. Fly shunting was used. As the engine went down into the yard it braked so as to slacken the couplings and allow the guard to release the locomotive. The driver then opened the regulator and the engine shot forward into a siding, the points were thrown over for the train to go by, the guard jumping into his van and screwing the brake on.

Quite a number of coal merchants had their own wagons: C.W. Jones, H. Wilmot, H.H. Smith, M.M. Niblett, Cainscross & Ebley Co-operative Society, Rogers & Dennis Ltd (their wagons were yellow, an unusual choice for a coal merchant), William Playne & Co., Longfords Mill, Henry Heaven. Coal came mainly from the Forest of Dean: Norchard, Cannop, Holly Bank, Lightmoor, E. Jarret & Co., Bowson, Dean Forest Coal Company. Stroud Gas Light & Coke Company wagons brought coke to Nailsworth for domestic boilers. Lippy's had a truck of coke every two months or so while the Purified Flock & Bedding Company and William Playne wagons carried small coal for mill boilers. During World War I some landgirls were asked by the farmer employing them to take a horse to Nailsworth station to collect coal. Taking him at his word they only led the horse to the station and abashed, had to return for the wagon.

Salt arrived from Salt Union, Bromsgrove, in covered wagons for Hillier's bacon factory and was shovelled loose on to drays. Hillier's had three truck loads of pigs two or three times a week, this usually being the only occasion when 'foreign' cattle wagons were seen on the branch. Butchers received animals from Gloucester market, one to three wagons arriving on a Monday evening and the animals being driven through the streets at 7 pm. Cattle were sent away after Nailsworth market held on the last Tuesday in the month. The cattle pen siding was lifted by 1963. Pigs were driven through the streets from the station to the factory, sometimes escaping and causing trouble. Latterly they were driven in a vehicle from the station to the factory. Blocks of ice came by rail for Hillier's and were hauled to the factory by LMS cart. Ice also arrived for Nailsworth brewery, people buying it from the latter, wrapping it in red flannel to provide insulation and then made ice cream to sell. Hillier's received by rail sawdust for smoking the bacon and cans to pack the produce in. Black puddings were dispatched in large, rope-handled baskets, so heavy that it required two men to shift only one. Horses were brought up the branch for Nailsworth Horse Show on the Tuesday following August Bank Holiday and showmen's vehicles occasionally used the station, for instance Hill's chairoplanes arrived by rail for the 1922 Horse Show and were hauled onwards to the field by traction engine.

E.A. Chamberlain made leather board for lining the insides of cars and this was dispatched by rail. Coal for the factory arrived in the company's own wagons marked 'Empty to Princess Royal Colliery Lydney'. Paper arrived by rail for the firm, almost a trainload of waste paper being received at a time.

Nailsworth station buildings

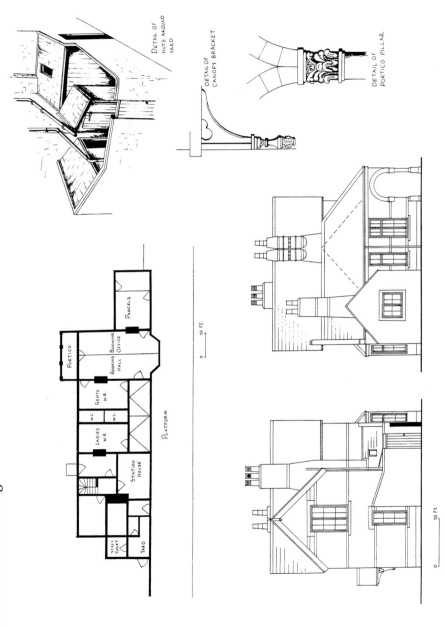

DETAIL OF
HUTS AROUND
YARD

DETAIL OF
CANOPY BRACKET

DETAIL OF
PORTICO PILLAR

PORTICO

BOOKING HALL

BOOKING OFFICE

PARCELS

GENTS W.R.

W.C.

W.C.

LADIES W.R.

STATION HOUSE

STAFF TOILET

YARD

PLATFORM

0   10 FT.

0   10 Ft.

0   10 ft.

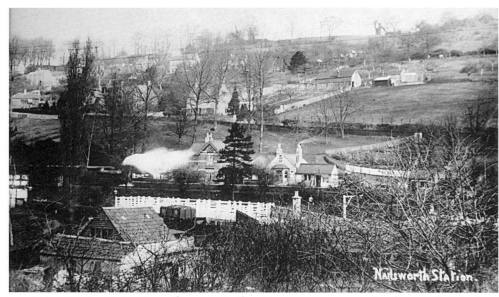

A class '1P' 0-4-4T at Nailsworth *circa* 1905. The picture was taken soon after the water tank had been resited. Note the panelling on the bracing supporting the tank, this panelling was later removed.   *P. Griffiths Collection*

Nailsworth, with the passenger station at the higher level on the right and the line to the goods yard lower right, while the water tank is on the left.   *Author's Collection*

The road to the station at Nailsworth *circa* 1905, with the goods yard on the left.

Author's Collection

Nailsworth station. Note the ground frame hut in the shadows on the left , the rack with three 'Stonehouse' boards for fitting to coaches, the inside-keyed rail chairs and the large tree on the platform.

Lens of Sutton

The Midland Railway Station.   Nailsworth.

Nailsworth station approach *circa* 1905.   *Author's Collection*

Staff at Nailsworth *circa* 1910.   *Author's Collection*

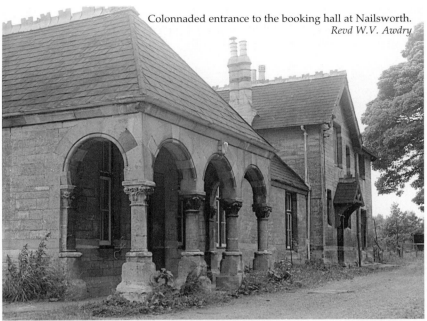

Colonnaded entrance to the booking hall at Nailsworth.
Revd W.V. Awdry

Details of corbels at Nailsworth.   *Revd W.V. Awdry*

Nailsworth station approach.

A.S. Apperley

Nailsworth goods shed, June 1966.

Revd W.V. Awdry

Nailsworth coal yard, June 1966. *Revd W.V. Awdry*

Exit from the goods yard at Nailsworth in 1965. *S.N. Adam*

EBBW VALE	CITY OF BIRMINGHAM GAS DEPT	MOIRA	COSSALL COAL CO	TWYNING	OLD ROUNDWOOD COLLIERY / WAKEFIELD
SETTLE SPEAKMAN	C. R. C. CANNOCK & RUGELEY COLLIERIES	GLANAMMON ANTHRACITE	WATH MAIN	ATKINSON & PRICKETT	ACKTON HALL FEATHERSTONE
LOCHGELLY	I. C. I.	THOS W. WARD KETTON CEMENT	JOHN BROWN	HICKLETON MAIN	WICKWAR QUARRIES WICKWAR GLOS
CHAPEL WHALEY & DISTRICT GAS COMPANY	WM PLAYNE & CO LTD NAILSWORTH	E.A. CHAMBERLAIN LD NAILSWORTH	THOS. W. WARD / T.W.W. LONDON	CHARLBURY OXON	G.L.M.
WIGAN COAL	SHIREBROOK MANSFIELD	PARKEND FOREST OF DEAN	E. JARRET & CO COAL FACTORS BREAM GLOS	KINGSBURY COLLIERIES LTD TAMWORTH	SHEEPBRIDGE
DEAN FOREST COAL CO	PRINCESS ROYAL COLLIERIES LYDNEY	DUNKERTON BATH	T. PAUL & CO LTD CLIFTON	ARTHUR PEPLER	BRADBURY
BALDWIN	BOLSOVER DERBY	S C	NETHERSEAL	C. W. S. BRISTOL	FIFE COAL
NORCHARD LYDNEY	BLAKE	GRIFF NUNEATON	CRUMP	WALSALL WOOD	HARRY GRIST WOODCHESTER
MATTHEW GRIST WOODCHESTER	JOHN GRIST ROOKSMOOR MILLS WOODCHESTER	GRESFORD	LIGHTMOOR	AUSTIN	BOWSON LYDNEY
STAVELEY SULPHURIC ACID	WHITWILL COLE & CO BRISTOL	THE PURIFIED FLOUR-BEDDING CO NAILSWORTH	TARMAC	ROADS RECONSTRUCTION	TYTHERINGTON STONE
G LOUCESTERSHIRE COUNTY COUNCIL	P. Y. X MALVERN	FOR PRICES WRITE TO EVESON LTD	HOLLY BANK	MILTON BRISTOL	GODFREY F. MEEK COLLIERY AGENT
COALPIT HEATH COAL CO BRISTOL	CLAY CROSS CAST IRON TANK MANURE	"COALITE" RADIANT SMOKELESS FUEL	SALT UNION LTD BROMSGROVE	STROUD GAS LIGHT & COKE CO GAS WORKS STROUD	CANNOP FOREST OF DEAN
CANNOCK CHASE STAFFS	WEST CANNOCK HEDNESFORD	CORY BROS LONDON	RICKETTS LONDON	UNITED STEEL CO ROTHERVALE KENT	RENWICK WILTON & DOBSON LTD
WM D FARRAR	BERRY HILL COLLIERIES	LAMONTE & WARNE	THRUTCHLEY & CO	GLASCOTE	AMINGTON & GLASCOTE
A. A. C. ANTHRACITE	AMALGAMATED ANTHRACITE SWANSEA	BEDWAS COKE	POOLEY HALL COLLIERY POLESWORTH	RICHARD THOMAS	ROSE RICHARDS
ANSLEY HALL	B. Q. C. ANTHRACITE	EVANS & BEVAN	BARNT HALL & CLELAND B. C.	NUNNERY	SHELTON
STANTON	WILLIAM MORRIS LONDON	BUTTERLEY	DICKENS & COX	OCEAN	COVENTRY
LLAY MAIN	BARGOED	READ & SON SALISBURY	SAXA SALT	FOR ... CEMENT BLUE CIRCLE	OLD SILKSTONE
DUNLOPS READING	SPUN PIPES CLAY CROSS	EDWARD CLOVER	BRITAINS BEST HOUSE FUEL OXCROFT	RADNORSHIRE	WILSON CARTER & PEARSON
NORTON & BIDDULPH COLLIERIES LTD	RICHARD THOMAS TINPLATE SHEETS	BAKER & MECHANICAL CARDIFF	LANCASTER DISTRICT COOPERATIVE SOCIETY	STAVELEY METAL SPUN PIPES	POINT OF AYR COLLIERY TAMWORTH
NEWTON CHAMBERS THORNCLIFFE IZAL	THOMAS SILVEY BRISTOL	JAMES SMITH STROUD	SHIVELEY METAL PIPES	REGERS & DENNIS LTD COAL NAILSWORTH	LANCASHIRE STEEL
H.H. SMITH COAL MERCHANT NAILSWORTH	SOMERSET COLLIERIES	H. WILMOT COAL MERCHANT NAILSWORTH	EXRS OF JAMES BESVICK	M.M. NIBLETT NAILSWORTH	W.Y. CRAIG & SONS
PEASE & PARTNERS THORNE	C.W. JONES COAL MERCHANT NAILSWORTH	STEWARTS & LLOYDS STEEL TUBES	BESWICK'S LIME WORKS BUXTON	LONDON BRICK CO PHORPES BRICKS	WHITE & BEEVEY
SMITH PARKNISS & COLE LTD BRADFORD	BEN CARTLIDGE BREWERY COKE CAINSCROSS STROUD	ROYAL LEAMINGTON SPA GAS COMPANY	STROUD LIGHTING & POWER	BLAIHILL	JAMES OAKES & CO EARTHENWARE PIPES

All wagons listed appeared between Nailsworth & Dudbridge late twenties & early thirties. Some only noted once, the majority in fact. Those coming regularly, apart from local owned wagons were from the Midlands (Staffs & Leicester), Somerset, and the Forest of Dean.

These wagons came on the branch between 1925-35.

In some cases the re-paying lettering must have lasted 10 years or more

C L N	B LN	WR	G N	L SWR

Private owner wagons which appeared at Nailsworth and Woodchester in the late 1920s and early 1930s.

Courtesy R. Woodward

Builder's plate on the goods yard crane.
Revd W.V. Awdry

Plates on the jib of Nailsworth goods yard crane.
Revd W.V. Awdry

The 1914-built Nailsworth goods yard crane seen in 1966. *Revd W.V. Awdry*

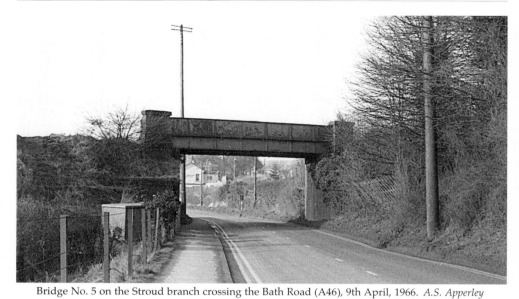

Bridge No. 5 on the Stroud branch crossing the Bath Road (A46), 9th April, 1966. *A.S. Apperley*

BR Standard class '2MT' No. 78004 climbing to Stroud from Dudbridge Junction and crossing the A46 on 12th May, 1965. *W. Potter*

Although waste paper and card continued to arrive by train, latterly the leatherboard was sent away by road. King's Engineering Works received rail traffic and steel plates for Newman Hender's which had to travel to Nailsworth because a crane was necessary to lift them off. There was a 5 ton crane in the yard and one of 30 cwt in the goods shed. Roadstone arrived in Gloucestershire County Council wagons as it was the last station on the A46 before Bath. Pyx, Malvern sent wagons of chippings for tarring. Other inwards traffic consisted of hay, straw, potatoes and building materials, while pigeons came to be released. Train loads of scrap aluminium left Nailsworth after World War II when aircraft were cut up at Ashton Down. Fish were sent away live from a trout farm at Horsley being transported in cans like large milk churns.

The station master lived in the station house and later took over control of Woodchester prior to World War II. At this period, other staff consisted of booking clerk, goods agent and clerk, two passenger porters (one on duty at a time), a man and boy on the weighbridge, a foreman in the goods yard, two shunters also acting as passenger porters and one junior porter. There were four LMS carters with four 4-wheel drays. Sometimes the four railway horses, shod by Joseph Smith, the local farrier and blacksmith, had to be attached to one wagon the hills were so steep. If they were particularly busy, a horse and wagon was hired locally.

About 1948 the animals were replaced by two Scammell mechanical horses. Later, a lorry which had taken over from the Scammells, was withdrawn about 1955, delivery then being the responsibility of the former GWR station at Stroud. In 1947 staff at Nailsworth consisted of a station master, part time woman clerk, two porters (one on each shift) who also sold tickets, a goods yard foreman and four draymen. The foreman did the shunting and was responsible for all goods in and out, ticketing trucks and sending goods away. Latterly there was only a porter in charge, assisted by another porter.

About 1900 a Mr Whiting walked to Nailsworth station each morning with a magpie sitting on his shoulder. As he boarded the train, the bird took wing, flying above the coach as far as Dudbridge, then returning to Nailsworth.

Stroud Branch

From Dudbridge Junction the line curved sharply round and climbing at 1 in 70 became single. Sometimes an engine slipped to a halt and the goods train had to be split, gasworks' coal being taken first. Near the summit was the Stroud Gas Works siding situated between Gas Works West ground frame at 104 m. 37 ch. and the East ground frame at 104 m. 56 ch. Although the Stroud Gas Light & Coke Company was established in 1833, coal arrived solely by canal until 1924, the last boat to use the Stroudwater Canal unloading 10 tons in 1941. An agreement for the siding was signed on 5th July, 1924, the gas company at its own cost and to the satisfaction of the LMS Engineer, constructing and maintaining the turntable, coal hopper and chutes. On 31st December each year the gas company was required to pay £1 for use of LMS

Above: Ground frame at Gas works loop.   *Revd W.V. Awdry*

Below right: Capstan for moving wagons at Gas works Siding.   *A.S. Apperley*

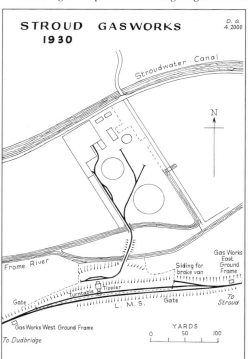

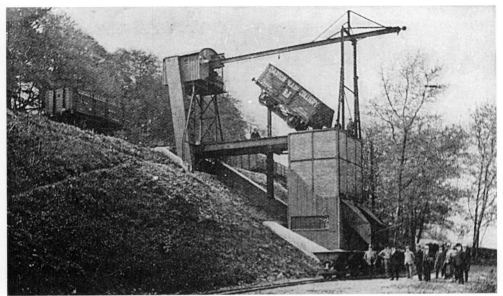

The coal tippler, Stroud gas works. Empty 2 ft gauge hopper wagons await loading. A standard gauge wagon is being tipped by hydraulic ram in Spring 1926. *Courtesy S. Gardiner*

Stroud gas works from the coal tippler. A 2 ft gauge petrol locomotive is pushing loaded hopper wagons. The two bridges cross the River Frome. *Courtesy S. Gardiner*

Stroud branch bridges Nos. 7 and 8, 3rd March, 1966.   *Revd W.V. Awdry*

Bridge No. 8 with its stepped parapet wall, 1963.   *A.S. Apperley*

land, the first payment being due on 31st December, 1925. The gas company undertook during the continuance of the agreement, to consign all its traffic for places served by the LMS, over that company's lines and also to use that railway for inwards traffic as far as it was possible to influence it. The siding laid by the LMS required the sluing of the main line to create enough room. The siding opened on 11th November, 1924. *The Stroud Journal* of 7th May, 1926 gave details of working:

> The trucks are run on to the top of a specially constructed chute, and instead of men being employed with shovels to unload the coal, the truck itself is slowly lifted at one end and the coal tipped into a large hopper, which is built on the edge of the railway embankment. The coal is then released through openings at the base of the chute into a series of small trucks attached to a miniature petrol engine, and run on rails direct to the furnaces underneath the gas retorts. By the arrangement, which was conceived and carried out by T.H. Woodcock (manager), a large amount of time and labour is saved. A very few minutes are required to empty a full 10 ton truck, and the whole of the work of unloading and transporting the coal is done by about three men.

A 2 ft-gauge railway was installed to convey coal from a loading chute of concrete served by the Stroud branch. The first engine was a petrol driven four-wheeler, replaced by a Ruston & Hornsby Ltd No. 183725 of 1937, bought second-hand from Joseph Pugsley & Sons, having previously been used by the contractor Edmund Nuttall Sons & Co. Ltd. Ruston & Hornsby No. 244564 of 1947 was bought new. The gas works closed on 31st May, 1956 and coal deliveries would have ceased a little before in order to run down coal stocks. Both Rustons were sold for scrap in 1959. The LMS branch was at a higher level than the gas works and a standard gauge wagon was turned on a table, run a short distance and hydraulically lifted so its contents were tipped out the end into a hopper which could then be released into a narrow gauge hopper wagon to go across the River Frome to the works. An electrically turned capstan moved standard gauge wagons along the siding. An average of seven to eight truck loads of coal were dealt with daily, or about 3,000 tons of coal per month.

Although the works closed in 1956, the Sectional Appendix to the Working Timetable published in October 1960 gave rules for operating the siding situated on a gradient. It stated that vehicles must not be allowed to stand on the main line at the siding without an engine being attached; wagons to be uncoupled at the siding were required to be marshalled next to the brake van, and this had to be placed in the siding built for this purpose. Points on the main line had to remain open for the sidings during the time trains were attaching or detaching.

The railway entered a cutting, passed under a 'stepped' blue brick bridge carrying Rodborough Hill over the railway, went under the Bath Road carried on a wrought iron bridge and at the end of the cutting came to double track. The line crossed the 145 yds-long Wallbridge viaduct on a sharp, check-railed curve. The viaduct is red brick inside, the bricks made by Samuel Jefferies & Son, Dudbridge, and blue brick outside. Some of the arches were walled up and let to businesses, Howard & Powell using a few arches as part of a cloth mill.

BR Standard class '2MT' 2-6-0 No. 78002 heading from Stroud with a goods train on 12th May, 1965.
W. Potter

Wallbridge viaduct, bridge No. 10, showing the beginning of the station loop, 3rd March, 1966.
Revd W.V. Awdry

Points at the Dudbridge end of the Stroud run-round loop. The photographer has his back to Wallbridge viaduct, August 1966. *D. Payne*

Wallbridge viaduct from ground level, August 1963. *A.S. Apperley*

Wallbridge viaduct, view up, August 1966. Notice Wallbridge Mill very close to the viaduct.
D. Payne

BR Standard class '2MT' 2-6-0 No. 78006 enters Stroud station on 7th August, 1964.
A.S. Apperley

Stroud station in September 1910.   *Lionel Padin Collection*

Stroud station, 105 m. 13 ch., variously called 'Cheapside' or 'Wallbridge', was situated on the north side of the line and held about four coaches. Its site is now part of the town's by-pass 'Dr Newton's Way'. The station, built of timber and with minimal decoration following closure to passengers was ironically occupied by British Road Services. Across the northern carriage way to the station was a board with title and the MR wyvern. In 1923 it was repainted with the LMS legend and no wyvern. In LMS days the platform nameboard was almost covered with red rambler roses - almost Midland red. Towards the end there was no station master, but in earlier times he used to live in a house at the end of Rodborough Avenue. Latterly most goods went to the GWR station, the grade 1 porter dealing principally with passengers. During the 1930s a joint delivery service was operated at Stroud by a 3 ton Scammell mechanical horse in brown and cream livery lettered 'GW & LMS RLYS'. After Nationalisation a porter was sent from the former GWR station at Stroud when a train came in for shunting. During World War II there were two women porters at Stroud LMS.

The goods yard was once very busy with a fleet of horse drays delivering groceries, timber, salt, agricultural produce, builders' materials and coal. Timber was carried from Sharpness Docks to Stroud and then about 1962 the railway raised the tariff and this traffic was lost to road, ironically lorries being off loaded on to land rented from BR. The timber-built goods shed with three covered loading bays after closure was used by a scrap merchant. The interior

Stroud track plan 1923

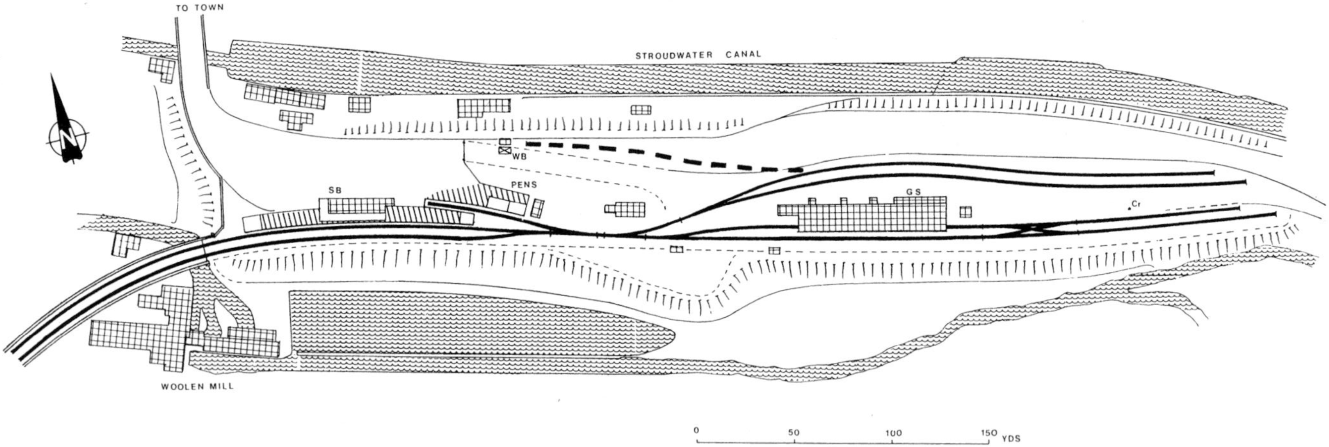

STROUDWATER CANAL

TO TOWN

WOOLEN MILL

SB

PENS

WB

GS

Cr.

0   50   100   150 YDS

Courtesy Peter Smith

Stroud station *circa* 1912, view towards Dudbridge. *Courtesy Railway & Travel Monthly*

Stroud station looking towards the goods yard, 3rd March, 1966. *Revd W.V. Awdry*

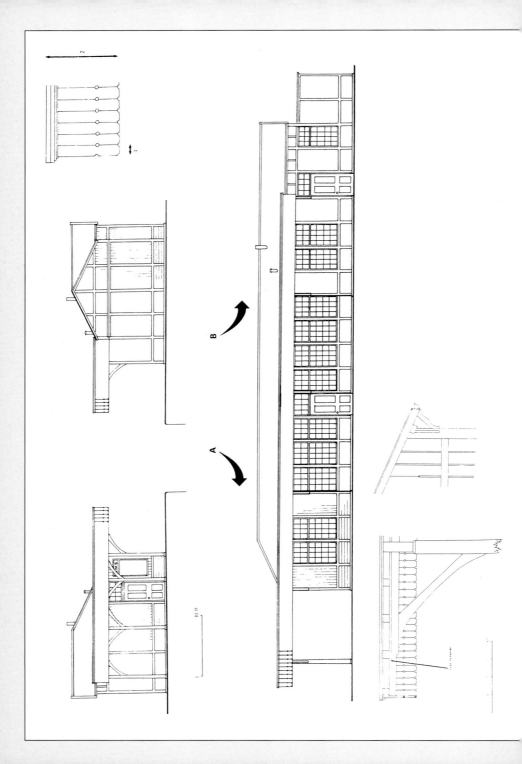

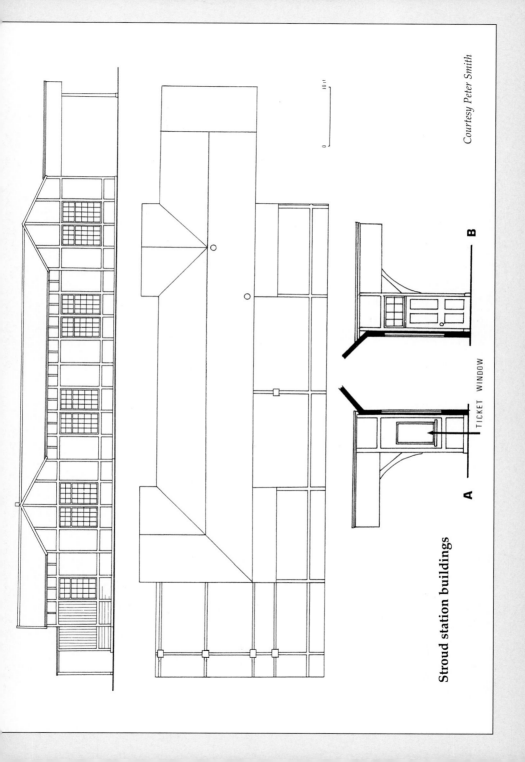

TICKET WINDOW

A

B

Stroud station buildings

Courtesy Peter Smith

Diesel-hydraulic type '1' No. D9500 at Stroud Wallbridge on 27th May, 1966.   *W. Potter*

Class '3F' 0-6-0 No. 43754 shunting at Stroud, view towards the buffers with the cattle dock on the left, 31st May, 1956.   *Author*

The bridge over the Stroudwater Canal taking the carriageway to Wallbridge station.   *Author*

Stroud Wallbridge station from the carriage drive, 3rd March, 1966.   *Revd W.V. Awdry*

Stroud, showing detail of the platform side of the station building in a state of dereliction. The booking office window is in the centre of the picture facing the photographer, and is unusual in being outside.   *D. Payne*

Stroud on 16th May, 1966. The view from the goods yard towards the passenger station. Notice the two three-way points.   *W. Potter*

was lit by sky lights. The timber-built office at the west end of the shed had a brick chimney. At periods during World War II the shed was full of margarine and was broken into and some stolen. Latterly the shed did not receive much traffic except at Christmas. East of the goods shed was a crane, while a public weighbridge stood near the entrance to the yard.

The MR Additional Powers Act 49-50 Vict. cap. 113 of 25th June, 1886 authorised the construction of a new road from the MR goods station, under the Great Western's Capels viaduct and across the Thames & Severn Canal to the London Road, opening access to the southern part of the town. Near the junction with the London Road was a two-storied building, the dray horses ascending a zigzag path to be stabled above the fodder stores and cart shed on the ground floor.

Diesel-hydraulic type '1' 0-6-0 No. D9535 at Stroud on 28th February, 1966.   *D Payne*

The Midland Railway stables, Stroud. Notice the steep access ramp. *Lionel Padin Collection*

GW & LMS Railways' 3 ton Scammel mechanical horse, in GWR colours, belonging to Stroud is seen leaving Bourne Mills of H.S. Hack of Brimscombe with a consignment of umbrella sticks.
Lionel Padin Collection

FROM **H. S. HACK**
WHOLESALE UMBRELLA STICK MANUFACTURER
BOURNE MILLS, BRIMSCOMBE, GLOS.

A COLONIAL CONSIGNMENT OF UMBRELLA STICKS LEAVING THE WORKS

W. Miles wagon No. 5. Painted black with white letters it was built by the Gloucester Railway Carriage & Wagon Co. in November 1892. *P.J. Smith Collection*

Samuel Jefferies wagon No. 7. Painted red with white lettering shaded black, it was built by the Gloucester Railway Carriage & Wagon Co. *P.J. Smith Collection*

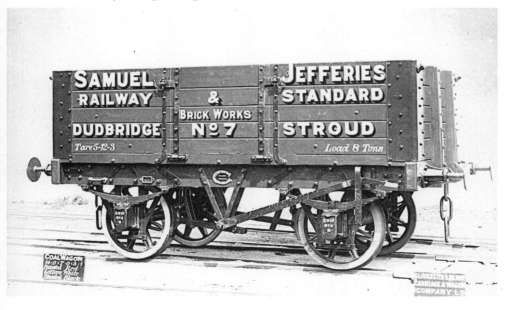

A panoramic view of Wallbridge goods yard from the GWR line on 15th June, 1946. The LMS goods is seen centre left, with the Stroudwater Canal on the right.   *L.E. Copeland*

Wallbridge goods shed in 1966.   *D. Payne*

Two views of diesel-hydraulic type '1' No. D9553 with empty coal wagons at Stroud Wallbridge on 16th May, 1966. In the view above the goods shed can be seen to the right. In the lower view the Oxford University Railway Society's headboard can be seen over the left buffer.

(Both) W. Potter

Dudbridge Junction on 28th May, 1947. Class '1P' 0-4-4T No. 1330 propels a one-coach train to Nailsworth. Note the junction signal. This was later replaced by a bracket signal.   *R.J. Buckley*

Class '1P' 0-4-4T No. 1390 at Stroud on the last day of passenger service, 14th June, 1947. *Left to right*: fireman, Tommy Knight; lady porter, Violet Tipton; driver, Charlie 'Cuckoo' Hickman.
K. Ofield Collection

Chapter Five

Closure

The decision to close the branch to passengers on 16th June, 1947 was made on the Government's instruction for a reduction in passenger mileage under the fuel economy campaign designed to help counteract the serious post-war fuel shortage. It was stated that it was not a permanent suspension, though the local press was informed that it would be for 'at least during the summer months'.

The *Stroud Journal* for 20th June, 1947 recorded the last trip in detail:

The obsequies of the 'Dudbridge Donkey' which made its last trip from Stroud LMS station to Nailsworth on Saturday night owing to the Government fuel economy campaign - prior to the 'temporary suspension' of the Stonehouse-Stroud-Nailsworth branch passenger service - were prolonged and by turns wistful and entertaining driver Hickman, of Gloucester, officiated on (and off) the footplate.

Notes of farewell had been sounding all day. Early in the afternoon one passenger admitted having travelled down from London on purpose to take one last trip from Stroud to Stonehouse via Dudbridge. The last train but one, scheduled to leave Stonehouse at 5.35 pm arrived at Stroud packed to capacity with boys from Wycliffe College Preparatory School, Ryeford, conspicuous with their scarlet caps and gay flags among the 'mourners'. Their farewells were 'cheering' ones.

The really big demonstration came later. The last train was due to reach Stroud at 8.4 and depart for Nailsworth at 8.6. Twenty-one minutes before this we approached the station with due decorum. But we were not first. Ahead of us was a man and his wife and just entering the station gates, another man. The couple sauntered along the station approach. The man did the same for a few yards, stopped, lifted his head, sniffed and dived into the just opened side-door of the Bell Hotel. He did not catch the train. Perhaps he never intended to.

On the station we found the couple sitting under the platform shelter and inside the booking office Miss Tipton, the last remaining lady member of staff, could be seen thoughtfully awaiting the last 'round up'.

The couple were Mr and Mrs E.J. Newell, of Paganhill. Mr Newell was a member of the station staff away back in 1908 under station master Edwin Allen, who actually opened the station on July 1st, 1886.

While we were talking to Mr Newell and taking a last look round at the station, and particularly at the special 'Excursion ticket' window, now closed for ever, many other people had gathered. It was 7.55 - nine minutes to go. Miss Tipton opened the normal ticket window and was soon doing a brisk trade in '9*d*. singles to Nailsworth'. As a special concession to the past the last two - numbers 300 and 301 - were sold to Mr and Mrs Newell. Our own ticket was No. 299 and we hoped to retain it as a souvenir.

The train was due, but did not appear. Instead there bustled on to the platform Mrs Dyer, of Upper Leazes. 'I travelled on the first train that left this station', she said. 'I had a lovely day at Speech House, and now I am come to see the last one go out'.

At 8.15 a taxi-driver joined the throng. 'The donk' he said 'left Stonehouse before I did, and I have been up to Belmont Road and back'.

It was getting a bit late. We asked Miss Tipton if she had any news of the train. 'I'll see if I can find out' she said. A moment later she was heard on the telephone. 'Is that Dudbridge; have you heard anything of the express?' Never had the donkey been so insulted.

Distant Rumbling

Soon there was a distant rumbling and at 8.24 - twenty minutes late at her own funeral - the train steamed in with pennants of red crinkled paper flying from the driving cab of the coach, where Mr Hickman had one or two young passengers. The engine was adorned with streamers of red bunting, on its front was the inscription 'Good-bye, Donkey' and on its flank similar phrases including 'Farewell Donkey, from Dudbridge LMS'. In the engine cab was the fireman and a young lady who had formerly belonged to the Stroud station staff.

Mr Hickman - 43 years on the LMS and seven on the branch - leapt with unbelievable agility from the control cab and dashed to the engine cab.

A press photographer wanted a photograph with the driver and officials standing around the engine. Steam began to pour from a valve at its side, enveloping the scene in mist.

'Can't something be done about that steam?' pleaded the photographer.

'Oh yes' said the fireman, and jumping into the cab he pulled a lever. The steam lessened, but it did not stop. Judicious blows on the lever with a heavy hammer had the desired effect, but this indignity was too much for the donkey. She almost burst with indignation, and probably would have done had not her pressure valve 'blown' just in time - to give the scene a cloud of billowing steam.

Everyone took their seats, and then left them again at the behest of the photographer.

At 8.31 the donkey began to move forward demurely, and we settled down to find out just how many bridges there were between Stroud and Dudbridge - that most expensive mile of railway. But we did not succeed owing to the distraction of watching people who had gathered on the embankment to bid a fond farewell to a fiery steed.

There was a Bang . . .

The pace slackened as we rounded the curving approach to Dudbridge Junction. There was a jolt. 'I hope nothing goes wrong on this last trip' remarked a lady passenger. Nothing did, but we thought for a moment it had. There was a bang, and another, and we rounded the curve to the accompaniment of a veritable crescendo of exploding detonators. Through the junction we dashed, and pulled up as a solitary bang signalled the limits of the journey in the direction of Ryeford. Then we nosed gently back to the 'up' platform.

The change of direction made it necessary for driver Hickman to change ends, and being a man to make the most of his opportunities, he bade an affectionate and demonstrative farewell to a number of alighting lady passengers on his way.

The whistle gave a short shriek, the 'swan song' of the donkey, for she never spoke again - at least she might have in deference to Mr Shinwell - and we were off. With the airy grace of a step dancer she negotiated the irregularities of the cross over, and scarcely had we regained our balance than, with an open road ahead, she was shewing us what she could do when she thought fit.

We crossed the bridge over Chumley's Drive (or should it be Cholmondeley's Drive?) at Woodchester with a veritable 'woosh', but peaceful penetration of Woodchester was prevented by excessive 'mining'. We ran into the station amidst explosions and cheers from a number of small boys. These, all carrying towels and what appeared to be pyjama suits, were the final passengers for what was positively the 'last lap'.

Nailsworth appeared strangely in different. Even the 'donk' seemed to sense this and sneaked into the station.

We disembarked with the intention of hurrying away without the legal formality of handing in our ticket. We had almost reached the barrier when a gigantic ticket collector, bare armed and brawny, held out his hand.

'Can't we keep it?' we pleaded.

'That you can't' he retorted. 'They have to go to Gloucester for audit'.

During this conversation four people had slipped by. That audit won't be very successful because outside they waved their tickets jubilantly. We hope Mr and Mrs Newell managed to retain theirs.

'What will happen to the donkey now?' we inquired of no one in particular.

'Oh she will go back to Gloucester as a light engine' someone answered.

Let us hope 'light' is the operative word. She deserves to take things quietly.

'Well goodbye' called out driver Hickman. 'We have had a good evening'. We had, and the donkey had reached the end of her career as a means of conveying sundry 'subjects of His Majesty on their lawful occasions'.

Footnote - Mr Newell wrote afterwards: 'This last ride was a little saddening to my wife and me. It aroused warm recollections of those days 40 years ago when life's serenity seemed somehow greater, and the locality's natural beauty was less disturbed by the insatiable encroachments of builders and industry.

'I am no classical scholar' he adds 'but I think the tag "*Sic transit gloria mundi*" is fitting'.

Closure to passengers was made permanent on 8th June, 1949.

The issue of the *Stroud News & Journal* for 26th November, 1965 said it believed that the last goods train on the Stroud and Nailsworth branch would run on 3rd January, 1966, revealing that a mechanised coal concentration depot would be built at Stonehouse. Then in April it was expected that freight on the branches would be discontinued about September 1966 on completion of the coal depot on the site of the down sidings at Stonehouse, Bristol Road, but in the event the branch was closed rather suddenly on Wednesday 1st June, 1966 in order that work on the depot could progress.

The *Stroud News & Journal* of 3rd June, 1966 reported:

A sad occasion passed unheralded on Wednesday when the last goods train pulled out of the old LMS station in Stroud *en route* for Nailsworth.

Nobody seemed to know much about the occasion and no-one cared. Our reporter heard of the event 20 minutes before and arrived in time to record history.

He went in time to see the train - 12 trucks and a diesel shunter - fade into the distance. There was one passenger on board with a sense of history and a camera slung from his neck, but nobody knew his name or where he came from.

Aware that he had a scoop on his hands and determined to follow his quest to the end, our reporter went in search of the man who organised the loading - Mr Merritt.

There is not so much to organise as the post is only part time. There is but one train every other day, and of course that's ended now.

Inquiries after Mr Merritt brought little response. But everyone knew 'Walter'. Assuming them to be one and the same, our reporter sought Walter's office.

It was very British Rail. An old iron stone, a kettle and a copy of the *Sun*. And Walter's coat, but no Walter. His sandwiches were gone too, which meant, apparently, that he would not be back until after lunch. He must have been on the last train.

The track was lifted by the time of the line's centenary in February 1967.

In 1973 Gloucestershire County Council bought for £200,000 the formation of the Stonehouse to Nailsworth branch including the spur to Stroud, as far as, but not including the Wallbridge viaduct. Between Stonehouse and Dudbridge the track formation has been used for a road which it is envisaged will be extended to the M5 interchange 13 at Eastington. Much of

An ex-GWR 0-6-0PT soon after arrival at Stroud with an auto-trailer with an enthusiasts' special in May 1952.   *M.J.E. Deane*

Another view of the pannier tank at Stroud in May 1952. The engine has now run round its train in preparation for departure. The fireman has yet to transfer the locomotive lamps to the bunker.
                                                                                M.J.E. Deane

Another ex-GWR pannier tank this time with the 'Severn Venturer' railtour on 15th April, 1956 at Stroud on 15th April, 1956. *W. Potter*

Class '3F' 0-6-0 No. 43754 taking water at Nailsworth on 31st May, 1956. *Author*

Class '1F' 0-6-0T No. 41748 is seen at Nailsworth with an enthusiasts' special on 25th August, 1956. Notice the nameboard in front of the photographer on the right. *C.H.A. Townley*

No. 41748 with the same enthusiasts' special on 25th August, 1956 at Stroud. *H.C. Casserley*

BR Standard class '3MT' 2-6-2T No. 82036 with an RCTS special passing Lightpill *en route* from Dudbridge to Nailsworth on 21st July, 1963.   *W. Potter*

No. 82036 near Woodchester with the RCTS special returning to Dudbridge on 21st July, 1963.
W. Potter

BR Standard class '2MT' No. 78004 taking on water at Nailsworth after wagons have gravitated into the yard on 12th May, 1965.   *W. Potter*

Class '4F' 0-6-0 No. 44264 passing the Stonehouse branch platform *en route* for Dudbridge on 30th June, 1965.   *W. Potter*

BR Standard class '2MT' 2-6-0 No. 78006 at Stonehouse returning from Nailsworth on 16th August, 1965. A diesel-hydraulic 'Hymek' locomotive can be seen on a main line down goods. Hoffman's siding can be seen on the right. *D. Payne*

Diesel-hydraulic type '1' 0-6-0 No. D9502 at Nailsworth on 2nd March, 1966. *D. Payne*

Local Trip Working—continued

BRISTOL 743
41XX Class Engine
Enginemen
Gloucester
743A 0425 **D** to 1225 **D**

Enginemen
Gloucester (Located at Stroud)
780 1045 **D** to 1845 **D**
781 1815 **D** to 0215 **MX** and Sunday

	arr.	dep.	
Shed		05‖15	**LD D**
Gloucester Old Yard ..	05‖20	0525	**(A) D**
Gloucester New Yard ..	0535	0600	**SX**
Stonehouse (Burdett Road)	0629	0632	
Stroud		0645	

Shunt and Bank as required until

	arr.	dep.	
Stroud		23‖00	**LE**
Gloucester Shed		23‖00	

A—On Saturdays to run direct to Stonehouse (Burdett Road) and Stroud.

BRISTOL 752
350 H.P. Diesel
Enginemen
Gloucester
752A 0720 **SX** to 1540 **SX**
752A 0720 **SO** to 1620 **SX**
752B 1500 **SX** to 2300 **SX**
752B 1540 **SO** to 2225 **SO**
758B 1735 **SX** to 2300 **MX**

	arr.	dep.	
Shed		0800	**D**
New Yard	0805	0833	**9F60**
Upper Yard	0838	0905	**9F60**
Barnwood Sidings ..	0910	Shunt 23‖00	**LD SX**
Shed		23‖05	
Barnwood Sidings ..		22‖00	**LD SO**
Shed		22‖05	

*Shedmaster to arrange 2nd man.

BRISTOL 753
Ex LMS. Class 4F 0-6-0 Engine
Enginemen
Gloucester
753A 0930 **SX** to 1753 **SX**

	arr.	dep.	
Shed		09‖45	**LE SX**
New Yard	09‖50	1000	**FRT 9**
Stonehouse ..		R	
Berkeley Road ..	1040	1115	
Sharpness ..	1130	1430	**FRT.9**
Berkeley Road ..	1500	1538	
Stonehouse ..		R	
Quedgeley ..	1605	1620	
Gloucester Eastgate ..	1643 GL	1729	
Barnwood Sidings ..	1738	17‖00	**LE**
Shed		17‖43	

BRISTOL 754
B.R. Standard Class 2 2-6-0 78XXX Class Engine
Enginemen
Gloucester
717 0240 **MO** to 1040 **MO**
558 0239 **MX** to 1039 **MX**
754A 1215 **SX** to 2100 **SX**
759 0845 **SX** to 1645 **SX**
759 0710 **SO** to 1515 **SO**

BRISTOL 754 (continued)

	arr.	dep.	
Gloucester Shed		07‖55	**LE D**
Loco Yard		08‖00	
Shunts Coal Stage and Loco Yard.			
Loco Yard		10‖55	**LE D**
Shed	11‖00		
Shed		1305	**LE SX**
New Yard	13‖10	1330	**FRT**
Coaley Junction ..	1400	1420	**FRT**
Dursley	1540	1600	**Q**
Coaley Junction ..	1620	1700	**Q**
Dursley	1720	1825	
Coaley Junction ..	1840	1902	**FRT**
New Yard	1938	2015	**TRIP**
Eastgate Goods ..	2030	20‖35	**LE**
Shed		20‖45	

BRISTOL 755
B.R. Standard Class 2 82XX Class Engine
Enginemen
Gloucester
755A 0655 **MWFO** to 1455 **MWFO**

	arr.	dep.	
Shed		08‖00	**LE MWFO**
New Yard	08‖10	0835	**FRT.9**
Stonehouse ..	0901	0923	
Dudbridge ..	0939	1006	
Stroud	1015	1050	**FRT.9**
Dudbridge ..	1058	1118	**FRT.9**
Newman Henders Siding ..	1145	1200	
Nailsworth ..	1207	1250	**FRT.9**
Dudbridge ..	1305	1320	
Stonehouse ..	1335	14*00	
New Yard ..	1431	14‖00	**LE**
Shed		14‖40	

BRISTOL 756
Ex L.M.S. Class 4F 0-6-0 Engine
Enginemen
Gloucester
756A 0440 **D** to 1305 **D**

	arr.	dep.	
Shed		05‖00	**LE D**
Gloucester Eastgate ..	05‖10	06‖00	**LD**
Shunts vans off 0350 Swindon			
New Yard	06‖10	0625	**TRIP**
Upper Yard	0630	0640	**TRIP**
Quedgeley ..	0655	07‖15	**TRIP**
New Yard	07‖40	0755	**TRIP**
Hempsted		0830	
Shunting	0830	1030	
Hempsted		1030	**TRIP**
Barnwood Sidings ..	1055		
Barnwood Sidings ..		11‖00	**LE**
New Yard	11‖15	1145	**TRIP**
Hempsted	1215	12‖45	**LE**
Shed		12‖50	

BRISTOL 757
57XX Class Engine **SX**
Enginemen
Gloucester
740 0300 **D** to 1100 **D**
757A 1030 **SX** to 1850 **SX**
757A 1030 **SO** to 1840 **SO**

An extract from the Working timetable 6th September, 1965 to 17th April, 1966.

Diesel-hydraulic type '1' 0-6-0 No. D9500 leaving Stroud for Dudbridge on 27th May, 1966.
W. Potter

A 350 hp 0-6-0 shunter D3994 arriving at Dudbridge from Nailsworth on the last day of operations, 1st June 1966.
D. Payne

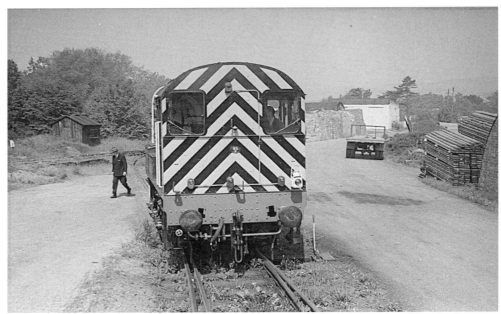

Two views of 350 hp 0-6-0 shunter No. D3994 at Stroud on the last day of working, 1st June, 1966. In the lower view note the narrow gauge locomotive standing in the yard and the embankment of the ex-GWR Swindon-Gloucester main line above the train.   *D. Payne*

the trackbed from Dudbridge to Nailsworth has been converted to a footpath and cycle track, while the central section of the Dudbridge-Stroud length has been put to the same use.

The severed west end of Wallbridge viaduct showing construction, 8th August, 1983.
Author

The main line side of Stonehouse signal box in 1966. *D. Payne*

BR Standard class '9F' 2-10-0 No. 92217 in the down refuge siding at Stonehouse with the signal box to the right, January 1965. *A.S. Apperley*

Chapter Six

Signalling, Permanent Way and Accidents

Signalling

Three signalling systems were used:

Stonehouse to Dudbridge Sidings signal box: staff and ticket: the aluminium staff being round and painted black.

Dudbridge Sidings signal box to Dudbridge Junction signal box: double line block.

Dudbridge Junction signal box to Stroud and Nailsworth: one engine in steam, with staff and key. The staff Dudbridge Junction to Stroud was triangular in shape and painted red, while that to Nailsworth was square and painted blue.

After closure of Dudbridge Junction signal box, a wooden staff box was screwed to the desk top in the booking office at Dudbridge station, this staff box being kept locked. The LMS signalling inspector kept duplicates of all three staffs in a cupboard of his office in the yard at Fishponds station, Bristol. The Stonehouse and Dudbridge Sidings staff had two pins to hold it in a rack in Stonehouse signal box. At Stonehouse, the porter in charge of the goods yard, or the train guard, was appointed to deliver the staff to the driver. When a ticket had to be taken while on the move the ticket was put in a slit on the end of a withy which had a string loop like a bow for the person collecting it to put his arm through. At the end of the branch platform at Stonehouse, one signal post bore the starting signal and distant for Wharf level crossing on one side, and Stonehouse up home on the other.

At the Wharf level crossing was a lever for mechanical communication between it and Vowles' (or Brushworks') level crossing. Before the Wharf crossing keeper closed the gates he was required to pull this lever which turned a lamp on a spindle. The Vowles' Crossing keeper indicated that he had closed the gates to road traffic by pulling a circular lever which turned a similar spindle and lamp near the Wharf level crossing. Later practice was for the fireman to open all level crossing gates on the branch, the guard closing them, a level crossing padlock key being issued to each.

Dudbridge Sidings signal box opened in November 1885 with 16 levers including two spare. A replacement box opened on 1st January, 1924. Manned by signalwomen in World War II, in 1945 they were paid £4 5s. 6d. per week and worked shifts from 5 am until 1 pm and 1 pm until 9 pm, though sometimes having to wait until 10 or 11 pm if the main line connection with the last branch train was running late. As the yard was on a curve, the points at the east end could not be seen from the sidings signal box, so a plunger was provided to indicate when to operate the points.

Dudbridge Junction signal box was opened in 1885 with 20 levers including four spare. A replacement box opened on 15th January, 1924. An engine whistled twice if going to Nailsworth and three times if going to Stroud. Until about 1947 the junction signal had a straight post with the top arm for Stroud and the lower arm for Nailsworth. This was then removed and replaced by an overhang

Interior of Stonehouse signal box in 1966.   *D. Payne*

Train staff in Stonehouse signal box.   *A.S. Apperley*

Signalman King (holding the Stonehouse to Dudbridge Junction staff) and leading porter Simpson at Stonehouse.
D. Payne

Staff and key box. *Front to rear*: Dudbridge Junction-Stroud, Dudbridge Junction-Nailsworth, Stonehouse-Dudbridge Junction.   *D. Payne*

Class '3F' 0-6-0 No. 43373 passes Dudbridge Junction signal box with the goods to Nailsworth on 8th July, 1955.   *Hugh Ballantyne*

bracket signal with upper quadrant arms on the bracket. Because of the up gradient, drivers liked a good run past Dudbridge Junction box and sometimes in order to help with this, the signalman came to the station with the staff. During World War II there was a signalwoman at this box and one fireman, knowing that his sister was on duty, put some grease on the staff before handing it over. The Junction box closed and the Sidings box was converted to a ground frame on 7th December, 1957 when the up platform road was taken out of use. The signals were removed at the same time. After passenger services had been withdrawn the signalman at the Junction box had plenty of time between trains and during the season went blackberrying within a couple of yards of his box.

Permanent Way

Single track was laid, but earthworks and most bridges were wide enough for double track. Between Ryeford and Dudbridge the track was relaid about 1935 with second-hand rails and sleepers from Wickwar tunnel. In 1955 between Stonehouse and Ryeford six to eight lengths of second-hand rail were laid in 1955-dated chairs on concrete sleepers put in by hand. Some rail joints on the branch were staggered. The branch was a Class 2 road and had clinker foundations with ash ballast on top, though about 1961 stone ballast began to be used for packing sleepers.

The permanent way gangs were based at Dudbridge and were supplied with a push trolley to carry their loads. One gang consisting of a ganger, sub-ganger and seven men maintaining both branches was split about 1950 into two gangs: a ganger and five men looking after Stonehouse to Stroud, while a ganger and two men maintained Dudbridge to Nailsworth. These became one gang again about 1957 and the reduction in traffic caused less wear and tear so latterly there were only two men and these were based at Stonehouse. In 1954 they worked from 7.15 am to 4.30 pm in the summer, finishing at 4 pm in the winter, still working an eight hour day by having a shorter lunch break. Duties, apart from keeping the track in repair, involved hedging and maintaining fences. Trees near Stroud had to be trimmed as they caused interference with the telegraph. Every Friday the gangers cleaned Nailsworth yard - picking up paper and weeds. The rubbish was dumped behind the goods shed and when enough had been collected, one or two wagons were sent from the permanent way headquarters at Berkeley Road. The men welcomed fog for the extra money it brought them going out on fogging duties, while in the days of passenger traffic, in snowy weather one permanent way man was stationed outside Dudbridge Junction signal box to salt the points. Latterly when the two-man gang was based at Stonehouse, the sub-ganger either walked from Stonehouse to Dudbridge and caught the bus from Dudbridge to Nailsworth and walked back, or went on foot from Stonehouse to Nailsworth returning by bus. He also used the bus one way either to or from Dudbridge to Stroud, and was re-imbursed his fares. In theory he walked the line each morning before the train came, though if he found cattle on the line, or broken fishplates which needed replacing, this would take first priority and the train might pass him. If it had snowed, he travelled on the train to clear any points of snow.

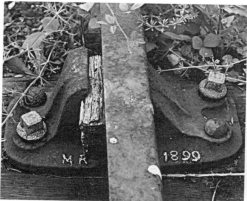

MR chair of 1899 on the Stroud branch.
Revd W.V. Awdry

LNWR joint chair of 1899 east of Ryeford.
Revd W.V. Awdry

MR chair of 1920 on the Stroud branch.
Revd W.V. Awdry

LNWR chair of 1921 at Rooksmoor.
Revd W.V. Awdry

BR (W) chair near Nailsworth.
Revd W.V. Awdry

BR 1955 chair on a concrete sleeper near Bridge
End.   *Revd W.V. Awdry*

Gradient post just west of the Bath Road bridge, Stroud. *A.S. Apperley*

Boundary post made from old rail and situated between Ryeford and Dudbridge. *Author*

Ground frame at Ryeford, June 1966. *D. Payne*

Point indicator at the far end of the passenger station loop at Nailsworth. Notice the goods yard
at the lower level.   *C.H.A. Townley*

Wheel stop.   *A.S. Apperley*

BR (W) chair left and LMSR chair right. Special fishplates join lighter rail section right, with heavier section, left.   *Revd W.V. Awdry*

If going along the branch to repair the track he went by bicycle and was allowed a travelling time of 20 minutes per mile for 'walking' from the point of booking on. Fishplate oiling and inspecting rail ends were the major jobs, but with only two and sometimes only one man, the branch could hardly be maintained to standard. Farmers complained of overgrown hedges, and brambles, sometimes going into a field for yards, which had to be cut. With only two men, not much work could be done on cleaning the cesses. Weedkilling pellets were spread in all goods yards by a 'fiddle', a hopper holding the pellets and a handle being turned to spread them. Weathering broke the pellets down and released a weed killing substance. Coal for permanent way cabins was unloaded from a train at weekends, but if they ran short and knew a driver, a shovelling action as the engine approached had the effect of getting the driver to throw some off. In latter days, instead of being paid at his base station, the area manager at Stroud found where a ganger was and came out personally, paying him on site.

Accidents

Fortunately no serious accident occurred on the branch. Class '1P' 0-4-4T No. 1730, (renumbered No. 1323 in 1907) ran through the stop blocks at Nailsworth on 19th January, 1892. The driver was alleged to be under the influence of drink and overran the station. In 1934 class '3F' 0-6-0 No. 3373 came off the road on two occasions at Dudbridge Junction going round the curve to Stroud. Blame was attributed to the permanent way and to the driver going too quickly. Eventually it was discovered that fault lay with a tender axle. Another class '3F' 0-6-0 casualty was No. 3754 which came off the road at Lane's Siding when on a non-stop seven minute trip from Stroud to Stonehouse with one coach. On 8th August, 1941 two British aircraft collided over the Woodchester valley. One pilot bailed out above houses at Inchbrook and landed on what was then the local sports ground opposite the Crown Inn, suffering only an ankle injury. His aircraft crashed into the railway embankment bordering the sports ground and burst into flames. The other aircraft involved, crashed into a field near Woodchester. It did not catch fire, but the pilot was killed.

Class '1P' 0-4-4T No. 1730 in the goods yard after a buffer stop collision on 19th January, 1892. Jones' builder's merchants warehouse can be seen in the background.   *Stroud Museum*

Derailment at Stonehouse *circa* 1952.   *P.Q. Treloar*

Chapter Seven

Locomotives and Locomotive Working

The first engines recorded on the branch were No. 110 a 2-2-2 built by Kirtley at Derby in 1856 and No. 2008; an 0-6-0WT rebuilt at Derby in 1871. In 1886 loads on the branch were restricted:

Double frame engines: 26 minerals; 32 goods; 48 empties
Single frame engines: 32 minerals, 40 goods; 50 empties

Railway & Travel Monthly for January 1914 records that Johnson 0-4-4Ts and Kirtley outside-frame 0-6-0s worked the line, three being in steam at a time on the branch and stationed at Gloucester Shed. Outside-frame engines were replaced by Johnson 0-6-0s with inside frames in the late 1920s. For the greater part of the period of passenger working, trains were hauled by Johnson class '1P' 0-4-4Ts. Ex-Lancashire & Yorkshire Railway (L&Y) engines appeared *c.* 1934, unrebuilt 0-6-0 No. 12141 and two rebuilt engines, Nos. 12131 and 12140, the latter having an LMS legend on the cab side sheets and the number on the tender, the other two having a number on the cabside and 'LMS' on their tenders. *Circa* 1930 an unidentified 2-4-0 appeared on the branch with no number on the smokebox door. This suggests that it might have been an ex-London & North Western Railway engine. The L&Y engines worked both passenger and goods trains. One fireman said that they produced black smoke all the time and were 'useless', while the class '3Fs' were 'free steamers'. In 1932 'motor train' working was instituted with the 0-4-4Ts. First was No. 1390 which had old-fashioned boiler mountings and returned to the branch after being rebuilt; No. 1303 was unrebuilt and No. 1324 rebuilt. Other engines recorded less often were 0-4-4Ts Nos. 1330 and 1364. Initially the locomotive pulled the train to Nailsworth and pushed it back, but later practice was to push to Nailsworth. This was because it was pushed from Gloucester. The auto-coach was brought out of a siding by the station pilot and put, uncoupled, behind the 6.25 am to Bristol standing at platform 3. The 0-4-4T came off shed, coupled on to the coach and after departure of the 6.25, pushed it to Stonehouse. The train normally consisted of only one coach, but two were used at busy times. On rare occasions when there were three, the formation was: 2 coaches, engine, 1 coach. Sometimes the 0-4-4T shunted a horse box or perishable van off a down main line stopping train at Stonehouse and trailed it up the branch, the formation being: coach, engine, van. The auto-engine and coach returning to Gloucester in the afternoon, often met the 3.32 pm Swindon to Cheltenham at Standish and raced it to Tuffley. In the last years of passenger working the auto-coach was left at Nailsworth overnight in the siding next to the water tank, the 0-4-4T bringing goods early the following morning picking it up. On arrival at Dudbridge it pulled forward to Dudbridge Sidings signal box, releasing an 0-6-0 which had hauled a coach from Stroud, the auto backing on and taking it to Stonehouse. One unusual visitor to the branch was a 'spinner' 4-2-2 which arrived with an inspection saloon in the 1930s.

STONEHOUSE, STROUD AND NAILSWORTH.

Miles.		1	2 Mineral	3 Freight	4 Freight	5 Freight	6 Freight	7 Freight	8 Light Engine	
			✿ a.m.	a.m.	p.m.	✿ p.m.	✿ p.m.	✿ p.m.	SX p.m.	
0	STONEHOUSE..✿...dep.	..	6 20	..	..	1 0	2 40	..	..	..
	Stonehouse Wharf	..	..	..	..	..	2 54	..	..	..
1	Ryeford........... { arr.	..	..	..	..	..	2 58	..	..	..
	{ dep.	..	..	..	..	..	3 20	..	..	..
	Lane's Siding	..	..	..	..	1 18	..	..	..	..
2¼ 0	Dudbridge......✵ { arr.	..	6 28	..	..	1 25	3 25	..	..	..
	{ dep.	..	6 39	9 8	12 45	1 30	3 37	4 55	6 10	..
1½	Stroud ....✿...arr.	..	..	9 13	12 50	1 35	..	..	6 13	..
4	Woodchester	..	6 53	..	..	..	3 51	..	..	..
5¼	NAILSWORTH ..✿...arr.	..	7 15	..	..	..	..	5 15	..	..

Miles.		12	13 Light Engine	14 Freight	15 Freight	16	17 I Engine and h. Brake	18 Freight	19 Through Freight to Gloucester	20 Through Freight to Gloucester
			✿ a.m.	noon	✿ p.m.		p.m.	✿ p.m.	SX p.m.	✿ SO p.m.
0	NAILSWORTH..✿...dep.	..	..	12 0	..	..	..	5 45	..	..
1½	Woodchester	..	..	12 25	..	..	4 0	5 55	..	..
0	Stroud ....✿...dep.	..	9 0	..	1 5	..	..	..	5 45	6 33
3¼ 1½	Dudbridge......✵ { arr.	..	9 3	12 30	1 20	..	4 5	6 0	5 52	6 40
	{ dep.	..	..	..	1 25	..	..	..	6 33	6 48
4¼	Ryeford........... { arr.	..	..	SUSP. Sats.	..	..	..	..	..	..
	{ dep.	..	..		..	..	..	..	..	..
5¼	STONEHOUSE ..✿...arr.	..	..	..	1 35	..	..	..	6 41	6 56

2—Arrives Woodchester 6.46, departs United Brassfounders' Siding 7.3 (detach only) and Dunkirk Siding 7.10 a.m. (detach only).   5—Arrives Lane's Siding 1.3 p.m.   6—Calls at Stonehouse Wharf when required, arr. 2.44.   Stops at Grist's Siding and leaves there 3.49.   7—Departs United Brassfounders' Siding 5.4 and Dunkirk Siding 5.10 p.m., attaches only at those places.   14—Arrives Woodchester 12.10.   On Saturdays leave at 11.45 a.m., Woodchester arr. 11.30, dep. 12.5 p.m., Dudbridge arr. 12.10, depart as booked.   Not April 8th.   15—Stroud Gas Co.'s Sidings arr. 1.7, dep. 1.17.   18—Arrives Woodchester 5.50.   On Saturdays departs Nailsworth 5.40 p.m., Woodchester arr. 5.45, dep. 5.50, Dudbridge arr. 5.55, dep. 6.0, Stonehouse arr. 6.10.   20—Leaves Stroud Passenger Station 6.37.

Freight timetable July 1939.

Between November 1941 and August 1944 SR 'K10' class mixed traffic 4-4-0s Nos. 137/8 were stationed at Gloucester, working the branch pick-up goods among other duties.

Class '2F' and '3F' 0-6-0s were used on freight duties until after World War II recorded engines being:

'2F' Nos. 3056, 3062, 3095, 3695
'3F' Nos. 3210, 3213, 3263, 3326, 3357, 3373, 3427, 3443, 3506, 3645, 3754

It was unusual to see an engine not on this list.

Occasionally a class '1F' 0-6-0T normally kept for the Dursley branch would appear on a goods train. After the war when traffic declined, class '4F' 0-6-0s appeared.

Engines which worked on the branch in the period were:

'3F' 0-6-0 Nos. 43213, 43258, 43337, 43344, 43355, 43373, 43464, 43468, 43506, 43645, 43712, 43754
'4F' 0-6-0 Nos. 43887, 43978, 44035, 44045, 44123, 44167, 44209, 44264

On 17th June, 1964 ex-GWR 0-6-0PT No. 8745 and BR Standard class '2MT' 2-6-0 No. 78005 appeared on a breakdown and goods train respectively. The first recorded sighting of a BR Standard class '2' 2-6-0 was No. 78006 on 24th July, 1963, other recorded members of this class being Nos. 78001, 78002 and 78004.

In the 1930s an excursion was usually just the ordinary branch train strengthened and hauled by an 0-6-0 rather than an 0-4-4T, passengers usually changing at Stonehouse into an excursion on the main line. Through excursions from Stroud and Nailsworth to Weston-super-Mare were worked throughout by one engine, usually a class '4F' 0-6-0, a passed fireman getting the job as driver. Excursion trains continued to run after the cessation of regular passenger services, the following being recorded:

Sunday 26th August, 1951	No. 44035 - 10.05 am Stroud and 10.40 am Nailsworth to Bristol (Temple Meads) and Weston-super-Mare
Sunday 29th June, 1952	No. 43978 - Nailsworth and Stroud to Weston-super-Mare (11 coaches).
Sunday 27th July, 1952	No. 40423 ('2P' 4-4-0) - special Nailsworth to Stonehouse to connect with excursion to Bristol (TM) and Weston-super-Mare (4 coaches)
Sunday 3rd August, 1952	No. 43887 - Nailsworth to Stonehouse to connect with excursion to Bristol (TM) and Weston-super-Mare (4 coaches)
Sunday 24th August, 1952	No. 40423 - 9.15 am special Nailsworth to Stonehouse connecting with Barry Island excursion (3 coaches)
Sunday 2nd August, 1953	No. 44035 - 9.15 am special Nailsworth to Stonehouse connecting with excursion to Weston-super-Mare. As the main line train was full on arrival at Stonehouse, the four coaches were shunted on to its rear.

Diesels first appeared on the branch in 1964-5, at first workings were interspersed with steam, but for the last 12 months of operation, the branch was

Class '3F' 0-6-0 No. 43754 taking the Stroud line at Dudbridge Junction on 31st May, 1956.
Author

Class '1F' 0-6-0T No. 41748, with '22B' Gloucester shedplate, takes water at Nailsworth after arriving with an enthusiasts' special on 25th August, 1956.   *H.C. Casserley*

solely diesel-worked. Normal engines were Paxman 0-6-0s (later class '14') diesel-hydraulic locomotives intended for short trip workings, The Paxmans had a poor reputation for reliability and were always breaking down, though no instance has been recorded of one actually failing on the branch. Engines recorded as working over the branch were: D9500, D9502, D9516, D9521, D9527, D9535, D9553.

Class '08' diesel-electric shunters were relatively rare on branch workings as their speed on the main line was so severely restricted (15 mph) and held up traffic. D3994 worked the last train on 1st June, 1966.

Prohibited engines on the Nailsworth and Stroud branches as at 1st October, 1945 were: London, Tilbury & Southend '2P' and '3P' 4-4-2T; North London Railway '2F' 0-6-0T; class '3' 4-4-0; L&Y '3P' 2-4-2T; LMS Standard '4P' 4-4-0; LMS Standard '4P' 2-cyl. 2-6-4T with parallel boiler (2-cyl. taper boiler allowed); '4P' 3-cyl. 2-6-4T and all classes 5 to 8.

Locomotive Working

An overall speed restriction was imposed between Ryeford and Dudbridge Sidings signal box of 40 mph and 25 mph elsewhere, but 15 mph between Dudbridge Junction and Dudbridge Sidings signal box. Engines worked tender first with goods trains from Gloucester to Nailsworth as they were then chimney first for the homeward journey and footplate crews were anxious to return to shed with all possible speed. Another advantage of going tender first was that a driver could see the train better when shunting. It was cold going tender first from Gloucester on a frosty morning and crews found the 8½ miles to Stonehouse quite far enough. A confident fireman sometimes filled the firebox at Gloucester, set the injector and went to sleep, though one of the dangers of this practice was that the boiler primed if it became too full.

Nailsworth was considered an 'old man's branch' in passenger days, for it called for no fast work and no night work and was therefore ideal for drivers nearing retirement and for whom trips on the main line might prove too strenuous. On the other hand, duties being relatively light, the firemen on the branch were often young, so youth and age were seen together on the footplate. Some drivers disliked the idea of having a young fireman left alone on the engine when it was propelling a motor train (unlike the GWR, he was not required to be a passed fireman), and either refused to take one out, or gave him precise instructions.

Train crews had their quirks. Charlie 'Cuckoo' Hickman was excellent at imitating the bird which gave him his nickname and often fooled passengers. One passenger guard always endeavoured to find an excuse to avoid uncoupling when an 0-6-0 needed to run round the train and tried to be busily occupied at such moments assisting with luggage, or telling passengers the time of a connecting train. One day an 0-6-0 was working the service all day as no 0-4-4T was available. It was during World War II and the guard had been kept on past retiring age. Normally the fireman assisted by uncoupling and coupling. On one occasion this guard climbed down on to the permanent way

Class '3F' 0-6-0T No. 47308 at the water tank at Nailsworth, having worked the Gloucestershire Railway Society Special on 7th July, 1963.   *W. Potter*

BR Standard class '2MT' 2-6-0 No. 78006 shunting at Nailsworth on 16th August, 1965.
                    D. Payne

Diesel-hydraulic type '1' 0-6-0 No. D9502 shunting at Dudbridge on 2nd March, 1966.

D. Payne

350 hp 0-6-0 diesel shunter No. D3994 coming off branch at Stonehouse on the last day, 1st June, 1966.   *D. Payne*

at Nailsworth to couple up and was distracted by a lady talking to him. He then climbed back on the platform and in due course waved his flag and the train set off. When the driver arrived at Woodchester he found to his mortification that there were no coaches - the guard had forgotten to couple up.

An interesting facet of drivers' behaviour is shown in that some cans of MR oil were found buried at Stonehouse. Apparently branch drivers at some period obtained the oil from a source to augment their supplies, buried them for a rainy day and then either forgot their whereabouts, or never needed them. Tank engines sometimes ran short of coal and the usual practice was to beg some from a tender engine. Signal boxes were rarely given a large enough coal allocation and footplate crews amplified it, one driver giving away so much coal, so rumour has it, that he had to borrow some from a merchant at Stonehouse. As a passenger engine did not stand stationary for long, many fireman adopted the practice of 'filling the hole up' and because of continual movement, the safety valves were not likely to blow off. Engines on the motor train took water at the up platform at Dudbridge every other trip though sometimes the auto-engine and coach did go down to the water tank in the goods yard at Nailsworth. Goods engines used Nailsworth water and were therefore less likely to use the water crane at Dudbridge. The water tank at Nailsworth was used as a railwaymen's unofficial swimming pool in hot weather. It was also used for fishing for pike.

Locomotive crews received various 'perks'. Bean sticks could be cut from the lineside at Nailsworth and Dudbridge; rather less honestly, one driver kicked off coal near Dudbridge and was rewarded with a box of eggs, another driver performing the same trick at the Ship Inn and was rewarded with a pint. Large lumps of coal were dropped out by permanent way gangers' cabins and they in return would provide bean sticks or rabbits. Logs could be bought cheaply from the timber mill at Ryeford and carried back on the footplate for domestic burning. A train sometimes stopped at Whiting's Crossing, just short of the Stonehouse branch platform for the driver to take a rabbit from a snare he had set earlier in the day.

Locomotive Sheds

From the opening of the branch a small timber engine shed was provided at Nailsworth on the east side of the goods yard at the foot of the embankment below the passenger station. Within six years the coal stage required replacement and the shed itself was in poor condition. By November 1895 it was disused and the MR Locomotive Committee recommended the removal of the water tank and coal stage. The water tank was re-erected by the goods yard. It was fed from a spring in the hillside north-east of the station. The turntable was removed c. 1920. A shed at Stroud was listed in 1892, but not mentioned in 1880 or in 1911 and no details of it are known.

Chapter Eight

Passenger Train Service

At first branch trains consisted of four-wheel coaches, six-wheel and bogie vehicles appearing later. About 1930 a close-coupled two-coach set put in a brief appearance. With the introduction of motor working on 12th September, 1932 only one coach was normally used. The first set used comprised first/third composite coach No. 3810 and brake third No. 1554, both converted for motor train working in 1931. At one period the pull-push coach was stabled overnight at Stroud, but latterly was brought down from Gloucester daily. It is recorded that the 'motor' coach was used on 30th December, 1944 was No. 24408. The coach for the tender locomotive working was kept at Nailsworth, while a spare strengthening coach was stored at Dudbridge on a siding opposite Dudbridge Junction signal box. When it was required the brakes were released and it ran to the rear of an up train by gravity. Vehicles exceeding 57 ft in length and more than 9 ft 4 in. wide were prohibited from using the branch.

The first timetable for the service which began on 4th February, 1867 showed three trains each way between Nailsworth and Stonehouse, two of the up trains taking 20 minutes and the other 25 minutes while all three down trains took 20 minutes. In April an early train was added - hitherto the first train had left Nailsworth at the rather late hour of 9.40 am, but one leaving Nailsworth at 7.45 am and returning from Stonehouse at 8.40 am improved the situation. These four trains continued to run on 1st July when Woodchester station came into use, the stop being added without increasing the journey time. The timetable remained basically unchanged until June 1880 when an additional train was put on leaving Nailsworth at 2.20 pm and returning from Stonehouse at 3.45 pm.

With the opening of the Stroud branch on 1st July, 1886 the timetable had necessarily to be re-structured. Nine trains ran each way between Stroud and Dudbridge, while the service was improved to seven each way between Nailsworth and Stonehouse. Apart from two trains from Stroud to Stonehouse, the method for working the other seven was that trains departed simultaneously, or almost simultaneously, from Nailsworth and Stroud and joined at Dudbridge to make one train from Dudbridge to Stonehouse, the procedure being reversed for down trains. By the time the July-September 1903 timetable was published the service on the Stroud branch had increased to 12 up and 13 down trains.

The timetable for November 1921 showed six trains each way between Nailsworth and Stonehouse and seven down and eight up on the Stroud branch. By March 1930 a train was running non-stop from Stroud to Stonehouse in seven minutes. On 12th September, 1932 when the pull-push 'motor' trains were started with no guard, the service showed four from Stonehouse to Nailsworth and four Dudbridge to Nailsworth with four Stonehouse to Stroud and five Dudbridge to Stroud. During World War II an early train was put on leaving Nailsworth at 6.18 am for the benefit of workers at Yate aircraft factory. The timetable of 7th October, 1946, the last to feature the branch passenger service, consisted solely of motor trains. They ran: four Stonehouse to Nailsworth; five Dudbridge to Nailsworth; six Stonehouse to Stroud and three Dudbridge to Stroud.

The Station in the Valley (M.R.). Nailsworth.
One of England's Beauty Spots.

Class '1' Kirtley double-framed 0-6-0 No. 2595 heading a four-coach passenger train at Nailsworth *circa* 1905. The train has been reversed for the benefit of the photographer to show the station buildings.

Author's Collection

A four-coach train in the up platform at Dudbridge *circa* 1905.   *Author's Collection*

Class '1P' 0-4-4T arrives at Nailsworth *circa* 1905 with coal stacked high in the bunker. Note the inside-keyed rail chairs.
Lens of Sutton

Class '1P' 0-4-4T No. 1364 at Nailsworth with a rake of 6 eight- and six-wheeled coaches *circa* 1910. Notice the point indicator at the far end of the loop. The engine bears the shedplate '7' which indicates Gloucester.
Author's Collection

STONEHOUSE, NAILSWORTH, AND STROUD (Single Line).

Miles from Stonehouse.	STATIONS.		1	2	3	4	5	7	9	10	11	12	13	14
			5.0 a.m. Mineral frm Gloucester.		5.30 a.m. Mineral from Gloster D	6.5 a.m. Mineral frm Gloster. F	Passenger	7.0 a.m. Mineral from Stroud.	Passenger.	Passenger	Through Freight. E	Passenger.	Passenger	Through Freight.
			a.m.		a.m.	a.m.	a.m.	a.m.	a.m	a.m.	a.m.	a.m.	a.m.	a.m.
..	STONEHOUSE		5 30	..	6 15	6 50	..	See page 428.	8 32	..	9 10	..	9 45	..
1½	Ryeford		..	..	..	..	..		8 37	..	..	..	9 49	..
2½	Dudbridge	arr.	5 40	..	6*23	6 58	..		8 40	..	9 17	..	9 52	..
		dep.	5 50	..	6*25	7 10	8 5	8 7	8 42	8 45	9 26	9 30	9 53	10 8
..	3½ STROUD		5 55	..	..	7 15	8 10	..	8 45	..	9 30	..	9 56	..
4¼	Woodchester	arr.	..	..	6 35	..	..	8 12	..	8 50	..	9 34	..	10 13
		dep.	See page 390.	..	6 50	See page 391.	..	8 17	..	8 51	..	9 35	..	10 16
..	Dyehouse Siding			..	See p. 391.		..	..	..	..	..	..	..	..
5¼	Dunkirk Siding			..			..	..	..	..	..	..	..	..
5¾	NAILSWORTH			..	6 55		..	8 22	..	8 55	..	9 39	..	10 20

STATIONS.		15	16	17	18	19	20	21	22	23	24	25	26	27	28
		Passenger	Passenger	Mineral	Passenger	Passenger	Passenger	Mineral	Light Engine.	Passenger	Mineral		Passenger	Mixed.	Stopping Freight. J
		a.m.	a.m.	a.m.	a.m.	p.m.	p.m.	p m.	p.m.	p. m.	p.m.		p. m	p.m.	p.m.
STONEHOUSE	dep.	..	10 37	..	11 12	12 10	..	12 40	..	..	S	..	..	2 23	2 35
Ryeford		..	10 41	..	11 16	12 14	..	..	..	SO	..	..	..	2 27	3 1
Dudbridge	arr.	..	10 44	..	11 19	12 17	..	12 46	..	..	..	..	..	2 30	3 6
	dep.	10 12	10 45	10 50	11 22	12 18	12 21	12 53	1 14	1 38	1 40	..	2 32	2 34	3 26
STROUD		10 15	..	10 55	11 25	..	12 24	12 58	1 17	1 43	..	..	2 35	..	
Woodchester	arr.	..	10 49	..	..	12 22	..	..	..	..	1 45	..	..	2 39	3 31
	dep.	..	10 50	..	..	12 23	..	..	..	..	2 0	..	..	2 42	..
Dyehouse Siding		..	..	..	..	..	..	..	..	..	P	..	..	..	..
Dunkirk Siding		..	..	..	..	..	..	..	..	..	..	..	..	..	..
NAILSWORTH	arr.	..	10 54	..	..	12 27	..	..	..	..	2 5	..	..	2 46	

STATIONS.		29	30	31	32	33	34	35	36	37	39	40	41	42	43	44
		Mixd.	Pass.	Pass.	Pass.	Pass.		Pass.	Pass.			Pass.	Pass.	Mixd.	Mixd.	
		p.m.	p.m.	p.m.	p.m.	p.m		p.m.	p.m.			p.m.	p.m.	p.m.	p.m.	
STONEHOUSE	dep.	..	3 55	..	..	..	..	5 52	..	..	..	6 35	..	8 2	..	..
Ryeford		..	3 59	..	..	..	..	5 56	..	..	..	6 39	..	8 7	..	..
Dudbridge	arr.	..	4 2	..	..	..	..	5 59	..	..	..	6 42	..	8 10	..	..
	dep.	3 24	4 4	4 6	5 16	5 19	..	6 1	6 8	..	..	6 44	7 17	8 12	8 14	..
STROUD		3 27	4 7	..	..	5 22	..	6 4	..	..	..	6 47	7 20	8 15	..	..
Woodchester	arr.	..	..	4 10	5 20	..	..	..	6 7	..	..	..	..	..	8 19	..
	dep.	..	..	4 12	5 21	..	..	..	6 9	..	..	..	..	..	8 20	..
Dyehouse Siding		..	..	..	..	..	..	..	..	..	..	..	..	..	..	..
Dunkirk Siding		..	..	..	..	..	..	..	..	..	..	..	..	..	..	..
NAILSWORTH	arr.	..	..	4 16	5 24	..	..	..	6 12	..	..	..	..	..	8 24	..

D—Stops at Dyehouse. E—Stops at Ryeford to detach important freight. F—Stops at Stonehouse Wharf and Lane's Siding. J—Stops at Stonehouse Wharf, Lane's and Grist's Siding.

YATE AND THORNBURY (SINGLE LINE)—WEEKDAYS.

Miles.	STATIONS.	1	2	3	4	5	6	7	8	9	10	11	13	14
			Empties. BX (See page 403.)	Passenger 9.26 a.m. ex Bristol. D	Mixed. B			Mineral	Empties. B Q	Mixed.	Empties. Q		Passenger 6.18 p.m. ex Bristol. H	
			a.m.	a.m.	a.m.			p.m.	p.m.	p.m.	p.m.		p.m.	
..	YATE dep.	..	8 37	9 52	11 27	..	..	1 15	2 35	3 10	4 40	..	6 45	..
2	Iron Acton	..	..	9 56	11 33	..	..	1 30	2 40	3 16	..	..	6 49	..
5½	Tytherington	..	8 50	10 2	11 42	..	..	..	..	3 25	..	..	6 55	..
7½	THORNBURY arr.	..	..	10 7	11 48	..	..	2 0	..	3 31	4 55	..	7 0	..

Miles.	STATIONS.	1	2	3	4	5	6	7	8	9	10	11	12	13
			Passenger to Bristol. (See page 382.)	Mineral. B	Passenger				Mineral to Westerleigh. B (See page 389.)	Passenger E	Mineral. B Q	Mineral. Q	Mixed to Bristol. S.P. 390.	
			a.m.	a.m.	a.m.				p.m.	p.m.	p.m.	p.m.	p.m.	
..	THORNBURY dep.	..	8 12	..	10 47	..	..	..	12 15	2 12	..	3 50	5 2	..
2¼	Tytherington	..	8A20	9 35	10 53	..	..	..	12 50	2 19	..	4 20	5 9	..
5½	Iron Acton	..	8 26	..	10 59	..	..	..	1 5	2 28	2 50	..	5 18	..
7½	YATE arr.	..	8 30	9 50	11 3	..	..	..	1 14	2 33	3 0	4 35	5 23	..

A—Arrives at Tytherington at 8.17 a.m. B—Bristol engine works these trips. All other trains worked by Thornbury engine. D—See page 415.
E—Runs as "Mixed" train on the second Wednesday in each month. H—See page 413. X—Does not exceed 34 wagons from Yate.

The branch timetable for July 1914.

NAILSWORTH, STROUD, & STONEHOUSE (Single Line).

WEEKDAYS

Miles from Nailsworth	STATIONS.	1 Mineral to Nailsworth.	2 Passenger.	3 Mixed.	4 Mixed.	5 Empties.	6 Passenger.	7 Passenger.	8 Empties.	9 Passenger.	10 Passenger.	11 Passenger.	12 Passenger.	18 Passenger.
		a.m.	a.m.	a.m.	a.m.	a.m.	a.m.	a.m.	a.m.	a.m.	a.m.	a.m.	a.m.	a.m.
..	NAILSW'RTH dep.	..	..	7 48	..	8 30	9 8	..	..	9 55	.	..	10 31	11 10
¾	Dunkirk Siding....	..	..	..		..		..	..	..	..			
	Dyehouse Siding....	..	..	..		..	9 11	..	..	..	..			
1½	Woodch'ster {arr.			7 52			9 11			9 58			10 35	11 14
	{dep.	7 0	7 50	7 53			9 12			9 59			10 36	11 15
..	STROUD				8 32			9 18	9 42		10 5	10 34		11 19
3¼	Dudbridge {arr.	7 8	7 53	7 58	8 35	8 40	9 16	9 21	9 46	10 8	10 87	10 40		11 25
	{dep.			8 1		8 49		9 22			10 11	10 44		11 25
4½	Ryeford {arr.			8 4		..		9 25			10 14			11 29
	{dep.			8 6		..		9 27			10 16			11 32
5¾	STONEHOUSE arr.			8 6		8 55		9 31			10 20	10 49		11 36

See page ...

	STATIONS.	17 Stopping Freight.	18 Passenger.	19 Light Engine.	20 Engine and Brake.	22 Passenger.	23 Passenger.	24 Light Engine.	25 Passenger.	26	27 Passenger.	28 Passenger.	29 Passenger.	29a Engine and Brake.
		a.m.	p.m.	p.m.	p.m.	p.m.	p.m.	p.m.	p.m.		p.m.	p.m.	p.m.	p.m.
NAILSWORTH .....dep.		..	..	..	..	..	1 25	2 15	..	..	3 5	..	..	..
Dunkirk Siding		..	..			..			..	..		..	..	..
Dyehouse Siding........		..	..			..		2 30	..	..		..	..	..
Woodchester {arr.		..	..				1 29			..	8 9			
{dep.		..	..				1 30			..	8 10			8 49
STROUD ...... {arr.		11 7	12 7	12 80	1 10	1 27			2 20			8 15	8 52	
Dudbridge {arr.		11 12	12 12	12 83	1 13	1 30	1 84	2 23	2 24		8 14	8 19	8 55	8 53
{dep.		11 86			1 20		1 87					8 23		
Ryeford {arr.		11 89					1 40					8 26		
{dep.		11 41					1 42					8 28		
STONEHOUSE .....arr.		11 48			1 25		1 46					8 32		

T Leaves Stroud Pass. Station at 8.50.

	STATIONS.	30 Passenger.	31 Passenger.	32 Passenger.	33 Through Freight.	34 Starts from Nailsworth Yard at 5.42, Staff Stage dep.5.45.	35 Leaves Stroud Passenger Station 6.40.	36 Through Freight to Gloucester.	38 Mixed.	39 Makes a trip to Stonehouse Wharf, when req.	41 Mixed.	42 Through Freight to Gloucester.	43 Empties, to Gloucester.
		p.m.	p.m.	p.m.	p.m.		p.m.	p.m.	p.m.	p.m.	p.m.	p.m. (T)	p.m.
NAILSWORTH dep		5 0	..	..	5 45	..	..	..	7 0	..	..	See page 414.	9 85
Dunkirk Siding		..	..	..		..			..	..	..		See p. 416.
Dyehouse Siding....		..	..	..		..			..	..	..		
Woodchester {arr.		5 4	..	..	5 50	..			..	..	..		9 40
{dep.		5 5	..	..	5 55	..			7 5	..	..		10 5
STROUD ...... {arr.		5 9	5 10	5 52		..	6 38	7 3		7 55	8 45		10 10
Dudbridge {arr.		5 13	5 55	6 0		..	6 43	7 6	7 10	8 0	8 55		10 10
{dep.		5 18		6 10		..	6 55		7 15	9 5			10 25
Ryeford {arr.		5 21		6 15		..			7 18	9 10			..
{dep.		5 23		6 15		..			7 20	9 20			
STONEHOUSE....		5 27		6 25		..	7 0		7 24	9 25			10 30

TUFFLEY BRANCH.

		Min. a.m.	Min. a.m.	Min. p.m.			Min. a.m.	Min. p.m.	Min. p.m.
GLOUCESTER ...... dep.		10 25	11 0	5 15	TIMBER YARDS...... dep.		11 55	1 30	8 30
Tuffley Sidings		..	8 SO	5 50	Hempstead Sidings ..... arr.		12 0	1 35	8 85
Hempstead Sidings ..... arr.		10 40	11 15	5 55	Do. dep.		12 15	1 50	9 0
Do. dep.		10 55	11 80	6 20	Tuffley Sidings .... arr.		8 SO		8
TIMBER YARDS ..... arr.		11 0	11 85	6 25	Do. dep.		12*20	1 55	9 15
				8	GLOUCESTER ...... arr.		12 80	2 5	9 20

TRAINS—MIDLAND & G. W. Co. at GLOUCESTER.

MIDLAND FREIGHT	WEEKDAYS Mons. & Tues. excepted.	M a.m.	M a.m.	M a.m.	MO a.m.	MO a.m.	M a.m.	M a.m.	MO a.m.	M a.m.	M p.m.	M p.m.	MO p.m.		SUNDAYS a.m.	a.m.	a.m.	a.m.
Gloucstr Mid. d.		12 50	3 0	4 20	4 40	6 0	6 20	9 0	10 0	11 0	2 20	6Z 0	10 0	..	12 50	1 30	5 0	9 0
" T. Sids. a.		1 0	3 10	4 30	4 50	6 10	6 30	9 10	10 10	11 10	2 30	6 10	10 10	..	1 0	1 40	5 10	9 10

G. W. GOODS.		M a.m.	MO a.m.	MO a.m.	M a.m.	M a.m.									a.m.	a.m.	p.m.	
G. W. Yard .... dep.		3 0	4 40	5 0	15	5 30	9 40	12 0	5 15	11 40					3 0	5 0	..	
Barnwood Sidings.. arr.		3 5	4 45	5 20	5 35	4 5	12 5	5 20	11 45						3 5	5 5	..	

Engines working these Trips to return immediately they are liberated.

D—If not ready to leave at 11.55 p.m. to be kept back by G. W. Co. until 12.55 a.m.
E—Works up the G. W. main line to Mill Stream Junc. and backs into the Yard when it is not convenient to accept it direct into the New Yard. G. W. transfer trips from Gloucester Old Yard to Mid. Yard at Barnwood will be limited to 40 wagons, and Mid. transfer to G. W. Yard will be limited to 35 wagons. Special trips to be run by either Company for perishable and other important traffic, as required, except that Transfer Trips from Gloucester (G.W.) for Barnwood Sids. (except with cattle) must not be accepted at Tramway Junction between 9.30 p.m. and 11.30 p.m.

The branch timetable for July 1914.

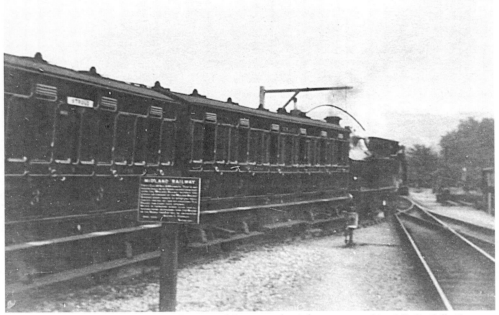

Stroud in September 1910, note the ground frame on the right.   *Lionel Padin Collection*

Class '1P' 0-4-4T No. 1361 at Stroud in the early 1930s.   *D. Thompson*

STONEHOUSE, STROUD AND NAILSWORTH.

WEEKDAYS.

Miles.			1	2	3	4	5	6	7	8	9	10	11	12	13	14	15	16
			Empty Motor.	PASSENGER	PASSENGER	Empty Carriage 8.0 a.m. from Gloucester.	MOTOR		PASSENGER	Light Engine.		MOTOR	PASSENGER	Light Engine.	MOTOR	PASSENGER	Empty Motor.	
			a.m.	a.m.	a.m.	SO a.m.	a.m.		a.m.	a.m.		a.m.	a.m.	a.m.	a.m.	a.m.	p.m.	
0	254 270	STONEHOUSE ✝..dep.	7 10	....	....	8 18	8 30	....	...	...	...	....	10 0	10 40	10 55	....	....	....
1		Ryeford	..	..	..		8 34	..	..	..	..	..	10 4	..	10 59	..	..	..
2½ 0		Dudbridge ✝.. {arr.	7 20	7 52	8 12	8 24	8 36	..	8 46	9 8	..	9 36	10 8	10 50	11 3	..	..	..
1		{dep. STROUD ✝ ......arr.	7 25	7 55		8 27	8 40	..	8 49	9 11	..		10 9		11 5	11 8	11 8	12 30
4		Woodchester .... {arr.	..	..	8 16	..	8 44	..	..	..	..	9 40	..	..	..	11 12	..	..
5½		{dep. NAILSWORTH ✝..arr.	..	..	8 17	..	8 45	..	..	..	..	9 41	..	..	..	11 13	..	..
			..	..	8 21	..	8 49	..	..	..	..	9 45	..	..	..	11 17	12 37	..

WEEKDAYS.

		17	18	19	20	21	22	23	24	25	26	27	28	29	30	31	32	33
		MOTOR	PASSENGER (MIXED)		PASSENGER		MOTOR		PASSENGER	PASSENGER (MIXED)		MOTOR	Light Engine.	PASSENGER	PASSENGER 8.10 a.m. from Stroud.	PASSENGER		PASSENGER
		p.m.	p.m.		p.m.		p.m.		p.m.	p.m.	p.m.	p.m.	p.m.		p.m.	SO p.m.		SO p.m.
254 270	STONEHOUSE ✝..dep.	2 29	....	....	....	....	4 5	....	5 20	5 21	....	7 52	....	....	9 27	..	
	Ryeford	2 33	....	..	....	..	4 9	..	5 24	5 25	..	7 56	..	..	..	9 31	..
	Dudbridge ✝ {arr.	2 37					4 13	..	5 28	5 29	..	8 0	..	..	..	9 35	..
	{dep. STROUD ✝ arr.	2 39	2 42	..	3 39	..	4 15	..	4 18	5 29	5 30	6 42	8 1	..	8 20	9 36	9 52
		....	2 45	..	3 42	..		..	4 21	5 32	..	6 45	8 4	..		9 39	
	Woodchester .... {arr.	2 43	....	..	....	..	4 19	..	..	..	6 35	..	..	8 24	..	9 56
	{dep. NAILSWORTH ✝..arr.	2 44	....	..	....	..	4 20	..	..	..	6 36	..	..	8 25	..	9 57
		2 48	....	..	....	..	4 24	..	..	..	6 40	..	..	8 29	..	10 1

WEEKDAYS.

Miles.			1	2	3	4	5	6	7	8	9	10	11	12	13	14	15	16
			PASSENGER (MIXED)	MOTOR	PASSENGER	PASSENGER	PASSENGER		PASSENGER	Light Engine.		MOTOR	PASSENGER	MOTOR	MOTOR	PASSENGER	Empty Motor.	PASSENGER
			a.m.	a.m.			a.m.	a.m.	SO a.m.	a.m.		a.m.	a.m.		a.m.	a.m.	p.m.	p.m.
0		NAILSWORTH ✝..dep.	7 34	....	....	....	8 32	....	8 40	9 0	....	9 20	....	....	10 0	....	....	....
1½		Woodchester	7 38	....			8 36		8 43	9 3		9 24	..		10 4	..	..	..
0		STROUD ✝ ......dep.	7 42	7 44	..	8 5	8 40	8 40	8 45	..	9 28	9 30	..	10 8	10 20	12 10	1 45
3½ I		Dudbridge ✝ .. {arr.		7 47					8 48			9 33		10 8	10*28	12 13	1 48
		{dep.	..	7 49	..	..	..		8 49		9 34		10 9			
4½	254	Ryeford .... {arr.	..	7 52	..	..	..		9 37	10 12		
5½	270	{dep. STONEHOUSE ✝..arr.	..	7 53	..	..		8 49	..	9 38	10 13	
			..	7 56	..	..		8 52	..	9 41	10 16	10*27	

WEEKDAYS.

		17	18	19	20	21	22	24	25	26	27	28	29	30	31	32	33
		MOTOR	MOTOR	PASSENGER	PASSENGER	PASSENGER	PASSENGER	PASSENGER	PASSENGER	PASSENGER	PASSENGER to Nailsworth.	Light Engine to Gloucester.	PASSENGER	Light Engine to Gloucester.			
		p.m.	p.m.	p.m.	p.m.	p.m.	p.m.	p.m.	p.m.	p.m.	p.m.	SO p.m.	S p.m.	SO p.m.	SO p.m.		
	NAILSWORTH ✝..dep.	1 45	3 25	....	....	....	....	4 47	....	7 7	....	8 35	8 35	....	10 6
	Woodchester	1 49	3 30					4 51		7 11	..	8 40	..	..	..
	STROUD ✝ .....dep.	....	....	3 27	4 8	4 45		7 5		8 12		..	9 44	..
	Dudbridge ✝ {arr.	1 53	3 35	3 30	4 11	4 48	4 55	7 9	7 15	8 15		8 46	8*44	9 47	
	{dep.	1 56	3 38	..	..	4 49	4 56		7 16		8 49	..		10*18
	Ryeford .... {arr.	1 59	3 39	..	..	4 48	4 59		7 19		8 49	..
	{dep. STONEHOUSE ✝..arr.	2 0	3 40	..	..	4 53	5 0		7 20	..	8 50		
		2 3	3 43	..	..	4 56	5 8	7 15	7 23	..	8 54	8*50		10*20

The branch timetable for 12th September, 1932. The start of the motor train service.

STONEHOUSE, STROUD AND NAILSWORTH.

WEEKDAYS.

Miles.	For continuation of trains from junctions, see page		1	2	3	4	5	6	7	8	9	10	11	12	13	14	15	16
			MOTOR		PASSENGER		MOTOR		PASSENGER	MOTOR	PASSENGER	Light Engine.	MOTOR	PASSENGER		MOTOR	Empty Motor.	
																SO	SX	
			a.m.		a.m.		a.m.		a.m	a.m.	a.m.	a.m.	a.m.	a.m.		p.m.	p.m.	
0	342 370	STONEHOUSE ⚲ ...dep.	7 10	....	....	....	8 30	....	....	....	9 57	10 40	10 55	....	....	12 8	....	....
1		Ryeford	7 14	..	..	..	8 34	..	..	..	10 1	..	10 59	..	..	12 12	..	..
2¾ 0		Dudbridge ⚲......⚲ arr.	7 18	....	....	....	8 38	....	....	....	10 5	10 50	11 3	....	....	12 16	....	....
		Dudbridge dep.	7 20	..	8 12	..	8 40	..	8 46	9 36	10 6	..	11 5	11 8	..	12 17	12 30	..
1		STROUD ⚲ .... arr.	7 23	....	....	....	....	....	8 49	....	10 9	....	11 8	....	....	....	....	....
4		Woodchester ...... arr.	..	..	8 16	..	8 44	..	..	9 40	..	..	..	11 12	..	12 21	..	..
		Woodchester dep.	....	....	8 17	....	8 45	....	....	9 41	....	....	....	11 13	....	12 22	....	....
5¼		NAILSWORTH ⚲ ... arr.	..	..	8 21	..	8 49	..	..	9 45	..	..	..	11 17	..	12 26	12 37	..

WEEKDAYS.

	17	18	19	20	21	22	23	24	25	26	27	28	29	30		31	32	33	34
		MOTOR	PASSENGER (MIXED)	PASSENGER		MOTOR	PASSENGER	PASSENGER (MIXED)	PASSENGER (MIXED)	MOTOR		PASSENGER	PASSENGER	PASSENGER 8.12 p.m. from Stroud.	Will run until August 26th (except July 29th and August 5th).	PASSENGER	PASSENGER		
								SX	SO			SO				SO	SO		
		p.m.	p.m.	p.m.		p.m.	p.m.	p.m.	p.m.	p.m.		p.m.	p.m.	p.m.		p.m.	p.m.		
STONEHOUSE ⚲ ...dep.	....	2 25	....	....	....	4 5	....	5 21	5 28	6 25	....	6 33	7 52	....		8 55	9 52	....	....
Ryeford	..	2 29	..	..	..	4 9	..	5 25	5 32	6 29	..	6 37	7 56	..		8 59	9 56	..	..
Dudbridge ⚲......⚲ arr.	....	2 33	....	....	....	4 13	....	5 29	5 36	6 33	....	6 41	8 0	....		9 3	10 0	....	....
Dudbridge dep.	..	2 34	2 37	3 30	..	4 15	4 18	5 31	5 38	6 34	..	6 42	8 1	8 20		9 4	10 1	..	..
STROUD ⚲ .... arr.	....	....	2 40	3 42	....	....	4 21	5 34	5 41	....	....	6 45	8 4	....		....	....	....	....
Woodchester ...... arr.	..	2 38	..	..	..	4 19	..	..	..	6 39	..	..	..	8 21		9 8	10 5	..	..
Woodchester dep.	....	2 39	....	....	....	4 20	....	....	....	6 40	....	....	....	8 25		9 9	10 6	....	....
NAILSWORTH ⚲ ... arr.	..	2 43	..	..	..	4 24	..	..	..	6 44	..	..	..	8 29		9 13	10 10	..	..

WEEKDAYS.

Miles.	For continuation of trains from junctions, see page		1	2	3	4	5	6	7	8	9	10	11	12	13	14	15	16
			PASSENGER (MIXED)	MOTOR	PASSENGER		MOTOR	PASSENGER	MOTOR	PASSENGER	MOTOR	PASSENGER	MOTOR	PASSENGER		Empty Motor.		
							SO	SO	SX	SX			SO	SO		SX		
			a.m.	a.m.	a.m.		a.m.	a.m.	a.m.	a.m.	a.m.	a.m.	a.m.	a.m.		p.m.		
0		NAILSWORTH ⚲ ...dep.	7 32	....	8 32	....	9 10	....	9 20	....	10 0	....	....	11 30	....	....	....	....
1¼		Woodchester	7 37	..	8 36	..	9 14	..	9 24	..	10 4	..	..	11 34	..	..	..	..
0		STROUD ⚲ ....dep.	....	7 44	....	....	....	9 20	....	9 30	....	10 17	11 28	....	....	12 10	....	....
3¼ 1		Dudbridge ⚲......⚲ arr.	7 42	7 47	8 40	..	9 18	9 23	9 28	9 33	10 8	..	11 31	11 38	..	12 13	..	..
		Dudbridge dep.	....	7 49	....	....	....	9 24	....	9 34	10 9	10•20	11 45	....	....	....	....	....
4¼		Ryeford .... arr.	..	7 52	..	..	..	9 27	..	9 37	10 12	..	11 48	..	..	..	..	..
		Ryeford dep.	....	7 53	....	....	....	9 28	....	9 38	10 13	....	11 49	....	....	....	....	....
5¼	342 370	STONEHOUSE ⚲ ....arr.	..	7 56	..	..	..	9 31	..	9 41	10 16	10 24	11 52	..	..	..	..	..

WEEKDAYS.

	17	18	19	20	21	22	23	24	25	26	27	28		29	30	31	32	33
	PASSENGER	MOTOR	MOTOR	PASSENGER	PASSENGER	PASSENGER		MOTOR	PASSENGER	MOTOR	PASSENGER to Nailsworth.	Light Engine to Gloucester.	Will run until August 26th (except July 29th and August 5th).	Empty Carriages.	PASSENGER		Light Engine to Gloucester.	
												SX		SO	SO		SO	
	p.m.	p.m.	p.m.	p.m.	p.m.	p.m.		p.m.	p.m.	p.m.	p.m.	p.m.		p.m.	p.m.		p.m.	
NAILSWORTH ⚲ ...dep.	....	1 43	3 22	....	....	....	....	4 45	....	7 14	....	8 35		8 35	9 18	....	10 15	....
Woodchester	..	1 47	3 26	..	..	..	..	4 49	..	7 18	..	..		..	9 23	..	..	..
STROUD ⚲ ....dep.	1 52	....	....	3 30	4 8	4 40	....	....	7 10	....	8 12	....		....	....	....	....	....
Dudbridge ⚲......⚲ arr.	1 55	1 51	3 30	3 33	4 11	4 43	..	4 53	..	7 22	8 15	8•43		8•43	9 28	..	..	..
Dudbridge dep.	....	1 57	3 36	....	....	4 44	....	4 54	7 13	7 23	....	8•44		8•44	9 29	....	10•22	....
Ryeford .... arr.	..	2 0	3 39	..	..	4 47	..	4 57	7 16	7 26	..	..		..	9 32	..	..	..
Ryeford dep.	....	2 1	3 40	....	....	4 48	....	4 58	7 17	7 27	....	....		....	9 33	....	....	....
STONEHOUSE ⚲ ....arr.	..	2 4	3 43	..	..	4 51	..	5 1	7 20	7 30	..	8•50		8 50	9 37	..	10•29	..

The branch timetable for 1st May to 24th September, 1939.

STONEHOUSE, STROUD AND NAILSWORTH.

WEEKDAYS.

Miles.	For continuation of trains from junction, see page		1	2	3	4	5	6	7	8	9	10	11	12	13	14	15	16
				MOTOR	MOTOR		MOTOR	MOTOR		MOTOR	MOTOR		MOTOR	MOTOR		MOTOR		MOTOR
													SO	SO		SO		SO
0	23¼ 24¾	STONEHOUSE ⌀...dep.		a.m.	a.m.		a.m.	a.m.		a.m.	9 44		10 35	a.m.		p.m.	12 2		p.m.
1		Ryeford		6 55			8 20			9 18			10 39			12 6		
2¼ 0		Dudbridge ⌀...⌀ { arr.		6 59			8 24			9 52			10 43			12 9		
		{ dep.		7 3 1 7 28			8 25 8 40	9 25	9 53			10 45 11 10			12 10		12 32	
1		STROUD ⌀........arr.		7 31			8 32	9 28				11 13					12 35	
4		Woodchester { arr.		8			8 11			9 57			10 49			12 14		
		{ dep.		9			8 15			9 58			10 50			12 15		
5½		NAILSWORTH ⌀...arr.		7 12						10 1			10 54			12 19		

WEEKDAYS.

		17	18	19	20	21	22	23	24	25	26	27	28	29	30	31	32	33
		MOTOR	MOTOR	MOTOR	MOTOR		MOTOR	MOTOR		MOTOR	MOTOR	MOTOR		MOTOR	MOTOR	MOTOR		
															SO			
STONEHOUSE ⌀...dep.		p.m. 12 58	p.m.	p.m. 2 25	p.m.		p.m. 4 5	p.m.		p.m. 5 35	p.m. 6 30	p.m.		p.m. 7 52	p.m.	p.m. 10 5		
Ryeford		1 2		2 29			4 9			5 39	6 34			7 56		10 39		
Dudbridge ⌀......⌀ { arr.		1 6		2 33			4 13			5 43	6 38			8 0		10 43		
		{ dep.	1 8 1 18	2 34	2 11		4 11 1 22			5 45	6 39	6 50		8 1	8 17	10 44		
STROUD ⌀........arr.		1 51	2 17		1 17				5 47	6 42			8 4				
Woodchester { arr.		1 12		2 18			1 27				6 54			8 21	10 48		
{ dep.		1 14		2 49			1 28				6 55			8 22	10 49		
NAILSWORTH ⌀...arr.		1 18		2 53			1 32				6 59			8 26	10 54		

WEEKDAYS.

Miles.	For continuation of trains from junction, see page		1	2	3	4	5	6	7	8	9	10	11	12	13	14	15	16
				MOTOR	MOTOR	MOTOR		MOTOR	MOTOR	MOTOR	MOTOR		MOTOR	Empty Motor to Gloucester	Empty Motor to Gloucester		MOTOR	MOTOR
													SO	SX	SO		SO	SO
0		NAILSWORTH ⌀...dep.		a.m.	a.m.	a.m.		a.m.	a.m.	a.m.	a.m.		11 0	11 10			p.m.	p.m.
1¼		Woodchester		6 18	7 16			9 14		10 3			11 4				12 22	
0		STROUD ⌀........dep.		6 22	7 20			9 18		10 7							12 26	
3¼ 1		Dudbridge ⌀...⌀ { arr.			7 14 7 21	7 47		8 35 8 38	9 30 9 33	9 30 10 10	10 12		11 8	11 28			12 30	12 41 12 44
		{ dep.		6 27	7 49				9 31	10 12			11*19	11*32				12 45
4½ 23¼		Ryeford { arr.			7 52				9 37	10 15								12 48
		{ dep.		6 31	7 53				9 38	10 16								12 49
5½ 24¾		STONEHOUSE ⌀...arr.		6 35	7 56				9 41	10 19			11*26	11*39				12 52

WEEKDAYS.

		17	18	19	20	21	22	23	24	25	26	27	28	29	30	31	32	33
		MOTOR	MOTOR	MOTOR	MOTOR		MOTOR	MOTOR		MOTOR	MOTOR	MOTOR	Light Engine to Gloucester.		MOTOR		Light Engine to Gloucester.	
												SX			SO		SO	
NAILSWORTH ⌀...dep.		p.m. 1 18	p.m.	p.m. 3 22		p.m. 4 45				p.m. 7 11		p.m. 8 35		p.m. 9 18		p.m. 11 8		
Woodchester		1 42		3 26		4 49				7 18				9 23				
STROUD ⌀........dep.			1 53 2 39		4 19		5 50 6 16			8 12		8 15						
Dudbridge ⌀......⌀ { arr.		1 56	1 56 2 42	3 30	4 22	4 53 5 55 6 19			7 22		8 15		9 28				
		{ dep.	1 57	3 30		4 54 5 54			7 25		8*43		9 29		11*16		
Ryeford { arr.		2 0		3 39		4 57 5 58			7 26				9 32				
{ dep.		2 1		3 40		4 58 5 59			7 27				9 33				
STONEHOUSE ⌀...arr.		2 4		3 43		5 1 6 3			7 30		8*50		9 37		11*21		

The branch timetable for 7th October, 1946 to 15th June, 1947. The last passenger timetable.

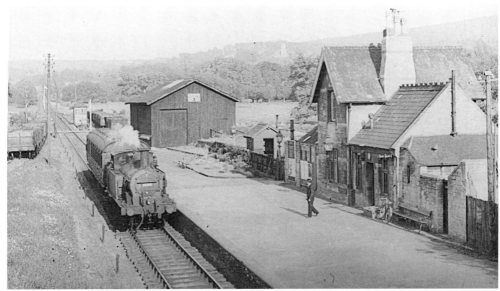

Class '1P' 0-4-4T No. 1330 arrives at Ryeford on a Stroud-Stonehouse train on 28th May, 1947. Notice the unusually wide platform, grain store and signal box.   *R.J. Buckley*

Class '1P' 0-4-4T No. 1330 and train from Stroud at Stonehouse, 28th May, 1947. Notice the point indicator on the left.   *R.J. Buckley*

Excursions and other features

A postcard with a ½*d.* stamp was posted at Stroud on 21st August, 1888 and reached Stroud MR station before 3.30 pm the same day bearing the message:

> France Lynch
> Stroud
> 21.8.88

Dear Sir,
  I proposed bringing my choir (16-18 wholes) down by the 9.55 am for Clifton, as quoted the other day, at fare and a quarter.
  Could you kindly have a couple of compartments reserved for us at Gloucester. It's no joke either for Passengers or the Co. to have a pack of boys in by themselves; and if you could tell me on my arrival could we book to Bristol & return to Mangotsfield, or to Clifton and change at Bristol?
  J.C. Kerry

At 3.38 pm on 21st August station master Allen sent a telegram to E.M. Needham, passenger superintendent, Derby: 'May I quote fare and quarter for France Lynch Choir outing to Clifton Down tomorrow. Party about sixteen thirds'. At 7.30 pm that evening Allen sent a telegram to Gloucester: 'Reserve two third compartments in your 10.2 am tomorrow for France Lynch Choir Stonehouse to Fishponds'. At 8.30 am on 22nd August Allen received the telegram from Needham (permission had been granted on the 21st, but the telegram was not sent until the 22nd), 'You may issue fare and quarter tickets to France Lynch Choir to Cliftondown [*sic*] tomorrow'.

On 2nd October, 1888 station master Allen of Stroud sent the following telegram to station master Pendry of Nailsworth. 'Three roof lamps out in 6.46 ex Stonehouse tonight for want of wicking. Please take up sharply with your men as we had enough of their slovenly work last year and a deal of annoyance was caused thereby. 7.55 pm C.A. Allen'. The following day Pendry sent a telegram to Allen:

Dear Sir
  I am looking after my lampmen and hope to prevent such neglect in future. If these are the only causes you have had this season, you are more fortunate than we have been, as I have *repeatedly* had to change two or three lamps in the Stonehouse portion of the 7.2 pm hence owing to your lamps not being trimmed and could not be lighted. Give your man a word or two as well please. Pendry.

In 1923 Mr Kimmins was issued with a trader's annual season ticket valid from Dudbridge to Stroud, Cheltenham and Bristol for £27 12*s.* In November 1925 a monthly season ticket was issued from Dudbridge to Dursley for £1 14*s.* In the 1940s about six season ticket holders purchased tickets at Dudbridge and additionally there were some at Stroud and Nailsworth stations.

Eight- to ten-coach excursions were run from Stroud and Nailsworth in 1935-6, on occasion having to be run in no less than three parts as they were so well patronised. An engine working a through train from Nailsworth or Stroud to Weston-super-Mare at Stonehouse ran on to the up main, uncoupled, and

Above: A Midland Railway excursion ticket issued on 7th August, 1888.

Right: A newspaper advertisement of 14th July, 1893 for excursion trains.

RAILWAY ARRANGEMENTS.

MIDLAND RAILWAY.
CHEAP EXCURSIONS.

EVERY MONDAY, THURSDAY, & SATURDAY,
until further notice, to

SHARPNESS, leaving Nailsworth at 9.50 a.m. and 1.15 p.m.; Woodchester, 9.55 a.m. and 1.20 p.m.; Stroud, 9.59 a.m. and 1.15 p.m.; Dudbridge, 10.7 a.m. and 1.25 p.m.; and Ryeford at 10.10 a.m. and 1.30 p.m. Returning each day from Sharpness at 6.55 p.m.

EVERY MONDAY AND THURSDAY
until further notice, to

SEVERN BRIDGE, LYDNEY, SPEECH HOUSE ROAD, COLEFORD, & LYDBROOK JUNCTION; (day trips), leaving Nailsworth at 7.53 and 9.50, Woodchester, 7.48 and 9.55; Stroud, 7.53 and 9.59; Dudbridge, 8.5 and 10.7; and Ryeford 8.9 and 10.10 a.m.

EVERY MONDAY until further notice, to

BRISTOL, BATH, WESTON-SUPER-MARE, CLEVEDON, CHEDDAR, and WELLS, (day trip), leaving Nailsworth at 7.53; Woodchester, 7.58; Stroud, 7.53; Dudbridge, 8.3; and Ryeford 8.8 a.m.   77B

GRAND FETE AT DURSLEY.

ON SATURDAY, July 22nd, to DURSLEY, leaving Nailsworth at 1.15; Woodchester, 1.30; Dudbridge, 1.27; and Ryeford at 1.32 p.m. Returning same day from Dursley at 10.0 p.m.   147A

ON SATURDAY, July 22nd, to BRISTOL, BATH, WESTON-SUPER-MARE, CLEVEDON, CHEDDAR, and WELLS, (day trip), leaving Stroud at 7.30; Dudbridge, 7.35; Ryeford, 7.40; and Stonehouse at 7.45 a.m.   147A

For full particulars see Bills to be had at the stations

GEO. H. TURNER, General Manager.

Derby, July, 1893.

proceeded to Standish Junction to cross over and come back to Stonehouse where it crossed over to the up main and coupled on to its train in order to draw it to the down main. Friday evening excursions were run from Nailsworth to Weston-super-Mare for 1s. 6d. return giving about four hours at the resort and arriving back about midnight. This inspired H.G. Creed to write:

The Age of Speed

We have a Railway service
At Nailsworth, as you know,
It's called the 'Dudbridge Donkey'
Because it travels slow.

A Nailsworth party boarded her
(Bristol their destination),
And everything was going grand
They changed at Stonehouse station.

Night came on, the train arrived,
The journey back to make,
The weary party jumped inside,
'Twas hard to keep awake.

And very soon a voice was heard,
A voice so very loud,
As up above the screeching brake,
It shouted 'Change for Stroud'.

The folks all tired and weary
Changed o'er to the other line,
And started moving once again,
So everything was fine.

But the change they made was far too great,
And they all began to weep,
Aboard the 'Dudbridge Donk' again
They soon fell fast asleep.

The 'Donkey' stopped at Dudbridge
(It isn't very proud),
And then instead of Nailsworth
We travelled back to Stroud.

Then back we came to Dudbridge,
When shunting had been done,
And then a place called Nailsworth,
And the battle had been won.

Now just a word to Nailsworth folk,
Travel how you like,
But if I go to Bristol again
I'll ride my rusty bike!

SPECIAL TRAIN TO

BRISTOL

AND

WESTON-SUPER-MARE

WHIT MONDAY
May 13th, 1940

| FROM | Depart | RETURN FARES (Third Class) | |
		To BRISTOL	To WESTON-S-MARE
	a.m.	s. d.	s. d.
GLOUCESTER	8 20	5 5	8 2
HARESFIELD	8 30	4 7	7 4
STONEHOUSE	8 40	4 2	7 0
NAILSWORTH	8A10	4 11	7 8
WOODCHESTER	8A14	4 8	7 6
STROUD	8A25	4 7	7 5
DUDBRIDGE	8A30	4 6	7 3
RYEFORD	8A35	4 4	7 2
COALEY	8 50	3 8	6 4
DURSLEY	8B30	3 11	6 9
CAM	8B35	3 9	6 6
CHARFIELD	9 5	2 6	5 4
YATE	9 18	1 2	4 4
	a.m.		
BRISTOL (T.M.) ... ... arr.	9 40		
WESTON-S-MARE (Gen.) ,,	10 16		

A—Change at Stonehouse   B—Change at Coaley

CHILDREN under three years of age, free ; three years and under fourteen, half-fares

PASSENGERS RETURN ON DAY OF ISSUE ONLY—
From Weston-super-Mare (Locking Road) ... ... 8. 0 p.m.
From Bristol (Temple Meads) ... ... 8.35 p.m.

Tickets may be obtained at the Stations shewn hereon, or at the Company's Town Offices and Agencies.

CONDITIONS OF ISSUE
Tickets are issued subject to the Conditions shewn in the Company's Time Table
For LUGGAGE ALLOWANCES also see Time Tables

All information regarding Trains on the London Midland and Scottish Railway can be obtained at Stations and Agencies, or on application to Mr. G. S. Rider, District Goods and Passenger Manager, 51, Victoria Street, Bristol.

April, 1940.   **T. E. ARGILE, Chief Commercial Manager**
(E.R.O. 53300)

2,000 H. 40 P.   Dawson & Goodall Ltd., Printers, Bath   3097

Handbill for an excursion to Bristol and Weston-super-Mare, 13th May, 1940.

Weston-super-Mare excursion at Dudbridge in 1949; class '3F' 0-6-0 No. 43258 leading, with another 0-6-0 as train engine.
Lionel Padin Collection

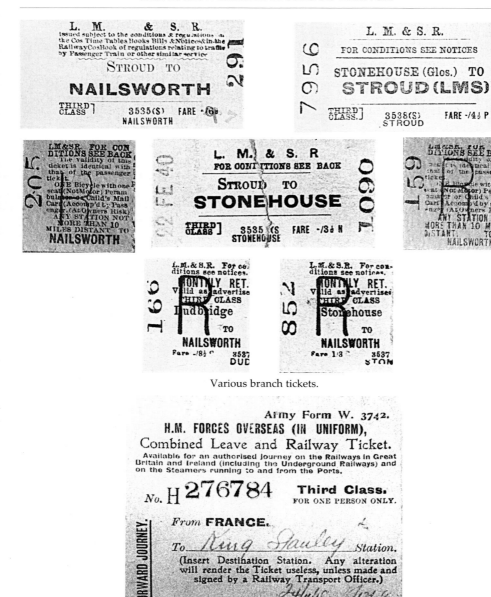

Various branch tickets.

World War I ticket from France to Ryeford (King Stanley [*sic*]).

A day trip to Portsmouth was organised and the four passengers from Nailsworth using the facility arrived late at Stonehouse after the last branch train had left. On asking the station master what they should do, they received the reply 'Walk'. After pointing out to him that they had purchased a day return ticket and that it was the railway's responsibility to carry them to their destination, the Stonehouse station master rang Gloucester Control advising them of the situation, but not revealing the number of passengers. This resulted in Gloucester sending a train of three or four coaches to carry four passengers. The Stonehouse station master had to rouse his counterparts at Ryeford, Dudbridge, Woodchester and Nailsworth to work gates and signals. On another occasion a party from Nailsworth went to a football match at Birmingham, returning to Stonehouse after the branch had closed. As they had paid to ride all the way back to Nailsworth, they felt fully justified in walking up the railway and much to their chagrin, found themselves accused of trespassing by the station master at Dudbridge.

When Forest Green was playing at Dursley in the local football cup final, a special supporters' train was organised, the distance being 12 miles by rail compared with only seven by road. Forest Green won the cup which was borne back triumphantly on the front of the engine.

Wycliffe College boys generally travelled first class on the branch and those of Marling School third class, though Wycliffe pupils were sometimes dragged into third class compartments by the grammar school boys. At Nailsworth boys made snowballs and took them in to the coach so that as the train drew into Woodchester, children waiting on the platform could be bombarded. Dudbridge station was used by pupils for Marling School, Wycliffe using Ryeford.

During World War II a nine-coach train of SR coaches arrived at Nailsworth with evacuees from Eastbourne. The train was so long that it had to draw up twice at the platform. Some passengers got out at Woodchester and were billetted there.

A typical day

Working varied over the years, but in the 1930s a typical day started with the first train on the branch leaving Gloucester at 3.15 am hauled by an 0-6-0 running tender first. Stonehouse signal box opened at 3.15 am to accommodate this goods. There was always a night turn porter at the station and he and the guard shunted the train out for various yards on the branch. It left at 5.10 am for Stroud, returning light engine and brake van to Stonehouse. Meanwhile another goods had arrived from Gloucester and on the return of the engine and brake from Stroud this goods left for Nailsworth. Having put the wagons in the yard, it drew two clerestory-roofed non-corridor coaches out of the carriage siding north of the station, the location of the siding being such that the engine had to run round the train in order to head it to Stonehouse. Meanwhile the first engine had followed, carrying the staff, with a load of coal wagons for Stroud gas works, going on to Stroud and picking up two passenger coaches. The 7.32 am mixed train ex-Nailsworth arrived at Dudbridge first and moved forward to Dudbridge Sidings signal box. When the 7.44 am arrived from Stroud the engine uncoupled, drew forward and backed over to the down line allowing the first train to back on to the coaches from Stroud, the lengthened train proceeding to Stonehouse where it connected with main line trains. It returned to Dudbridge where it split for Stroud and Nailsworth. The 'motor' arrived from Gloucester and worked the 8.30 am to Nailsworth continuing through the day until 7.07 pm from Nailsworth after which it returned to Gloucester. Throughout the day an 0-6-0 also worked passenger trains and also those in the late evening. Both 0-6-0s returned to Gloucester at the head of a goods train. In the latter days of passenger working, all trains were covered by one 'motor', it calling at Stroud *en route* to or from Nailsworth, this type of train being suited to so many reversals.

The Stonehouse to Stroud train approaching Rodborough Bridge (No. 8) in September 1937 pushed by Class '1P' 0-4-4T No. 1390.   *P. Strange*

Appendix One

Statistics of Nailsworth and Stroud Branches

Station	Year	No. of Season Tickets	No. of Passengers booked	Passenger receipts £	Parcels, horses, carriages, dogs receipts £	Total coaching receipts £	Goods debit £	No. of livestock trucks in & out	Coal, coke limestone in & out tons	Carted in & out tons	Not carted in & out tons	Minerals in & out tons	Tranships tons	Expenses of station
Stonehouse	1872	-	33,521	2,936	253	3,189		267	3,020	3,335	4,797	181	244	772
	1882	-	35,340	2,878	315	3,193		199	2,278	3,422	2,604	1,070	945	923
	1892	7	42,014	2,609	328	2,937		218	2,243	1,449	1,465	1,821	621	846
	1902	20	38,925	2,957	385	3,342	1,616	152	2,396	1,418	2,176	2,355	1,221	1,058
	1912	22	37,564	3,304	431	3,735	2,039	246	3,012	2,213	2,282	6,877	1,182	1,316
	1922	28	31,049	5,075	412	5,487	3,363	275	2,951	1,831	1,177	7,989	135	3,730
Ryeford	1872	-	10,006	273	22	295		15	1,455	173	20,633	196		146
	1882	-	11,385	234	30	264		6	3,253	258	10,940	401		155
	1892	13	28,600	469	36	505			2,984	900	2,815	743		253
	1902	15	22,778	540	108	648	1,997		2,752	938	3,848	535		253
	1912	7	16,478	355	57	412	1,640		1,959	778	1,942	2,628		280
	1922	32	10,856	508	441	949	3,053		2,902	454	2,230	1,089		598
Dudbridge	1872	-	23,807	809	477	1,286		6	5,501	1,627	9,387	814		178
	1882	-	31,976	1,233	442	1,675		18	5,836	4,387	5,783	1,067		256
	1892	10	41,964	968	113	1,081		69	10,119	661	9,346	2,598		449
	1902	12	38,299	847	191	1,938	3,271	137	10,054	859	5,804	5,688		562
	1912	16	33,495	981	242	1,223	1,464	254	11,715	383	2,974	2,781	72	666
	1922	5	18,665	1,291	899	2,190	3,687	244	12,715	1,036	3,334	1,192		1,494

Station	Year	No. of Season Tickets	No. of Passengers booked	Passenger receipts £	Parcels, horses, carriages, dogs receipts £	Total coaching receipts £	Goods debit £	No. of livestock trucks in & out	Coal, coke limestone in & out tons	Carted in & out tons	Not carted in & out tons	Minerals in & out tons	Tranships tons	Expenses of station
Stroud	1872											1,398	66	*
	1882	*No passenger statistics until 1896*					*Opened for goods traffic November 1885*						893	6	*
	1892							99	13,717	12,864	13,251	2,287	137	1,812
	1902	15	70,109	4,484	1,325	5,809	15,807	89	12,322	13,754	14,272	4,092	190	2,534†
	1912	14	55,023	4,020	1,466	5,486	16,222	125	9,992	14,878	11,959	4,824	751	2,512#
	1922	7	20,788	2,928	1,240	4,168	19,302	60	12,064	8,924	5,623	10,053	374	4,120§
Woodchester	1872	–	11,486	386	44	430			2,874	1,627	1,403	106		170
	1882	–	14,045	501	78	579			3,619	1,509	3,303	799		181
	1892	10	25,205	693	79	772			2,964	1,599	3,219	2,017		193
	1902	5	22,985	814	173	987	3,526		3,523	2,128	3,513	817		194
	1912	5	21,689	811	117	928	3,727		2,938	2,067	4,805	1,105		259
	1922	14	9,585	911	659	1,570	9,908		4,114	3,130	3,207	3,064		969
Nailsworth	1872	–	21,667	1,253	645	1,898		784	12,394	2,878	6,886	1,789		387
	1882	–	31,066	1,652	863	2,515		848	13,200	3,657	6,780	2,991		569
	1892	25	39,031	2,114	968	3,082		1,000	13,972	4,846	6,939	5,466		501
	1902	13	37,339	2,166	943	3,109	5,642	455	12,735	4,753	7,461	5,313		560
	1912	30	33,787	2,336	1,016	3,352	6,996	401	13,473	5,913	7,198	6,708		610
	1922	52	14,575	2,454	2,098	4,552	14,391	341	14,672	5,097	6,495	2,250		1,862

Notes: * Expenses included in Stonehouse   † Plus passenger station £312   # Plus passenger station £394   § Plus passenger station £679

Log of 8.15 am Gloucester to Stroud and Nailsworth Goods Train, 13th June, 1962

Locomotive: Class '4F' 0-6-0 No. 44167

0.00	Gloucester New Yard		8.12	MP97¾-98 23 mph
8.40	Stonehouse	8.37	8.47	Ship Crossing 8.51-8.58½
1.11	Ryeford		10.01	Passing time
1.23	Dudbridge Jn	10.06	10.20	
1.07	Stroud	10.25	10.52½	
1.07	Dudbridge Jn	10.58	11.11	
				lc 11.17-11.21
1.43	Woodchester lc	11.22	11.26	
0.64	Newman Hender's sdg	11.29	11.39	
0.57	Nailsworth	11.44	12.48	
1.41	Woodchester lc	12.55½	1.00	
				lc 1.01-1.04½
1.43	Dudbridge Jn	1.11	1.11½	
				Ship Crossing 1.17½-1.24½
2.34	Stonehouse	1.30	1.52	
				36 mph
8.40	Gloucester New Yard	2.10		

Class '4F' 0-6-0 No. 44167 at Nailsworth on 13th June, 1962.   *Author*

Driver Preece on class '4F' 0-6-0 No. 44167 at Nailsworth on 13th June, 1962.

Author

Acknowledgements

Especial thanks are due to Ken Ofield and R. Woodward who checked the manuscript and also to P.J. Smith for the use of his drawings which originally appeared in *An Historical Survey of the Midland in Gloucestershire* published by the Oxford Publishing Co. in 1985.

The following organisations and individuals also gave assistance:

S.N. Adams
B. Ashworth
A.S. Apperley
Revd W.V. Awdry
L.E. Bathe
A. Bennet
W.J.S. Brunt
R. Buckley
M.G. Burtt
P. Copeland
H.G. Creed
B. Davis
M.E.J. Deane
G. Dow
B. Edwards
E. Elliott
S. Fawlk
Mrs S. Gardner
Gloucestershire Record Office
Gloucester Reference Library
Miss E. Halliday
G.R.T. Harrison
A. Hammond
J. Hopkins
O. Jeffery
C. Jones
R. Kelham
T. Knight
R.G. Lawrence

R. Laker
A.M. Langford
Miss P. Lewis
Mrs G.C. Mills
C. Minnet
A.M. Morley, Stroud Library
H. Nabb
A.C. Newman
F.R. Newman
L. C. Padin
D. Payne
C.W. Pegler
G. Pothecary
W. Potter
B. Pugh
Public Record Office, Kew
Miss B.J. Smith
J.V. Smith
D.R. Steggles
T. Tanner
C.H.A. Townley
P.Q. Treloar
D. Viner, Corinium Museum
L. Walrond, Stroud & District Museum
C.G. Wells
S.J. Wilkes
G.J. Woodward
R. Wyman

Bibliography

Steam in the West Midlands & South Wales by B.J. Ashworth (Ian Allan, 1975)
A History of Woodchester by Revd W.N.R.J. Black
Bradshaw's Railway Manual 1869
Closed Stations & Goods Depots by C.R. Clinker (Avon Anglia, 1988)
Track Layout Diagrams of the GWR and BR WR Section 20: South Gloucestershire by R.A. Cooke (Author, 1988)
British Canals by Charles Hadfield (David & Charles, 1984)
Canals of South & South East England by C. Hadfield (David & Charles, 1969)
The Stroudwater Canal by M. Handford (Alan Sutton, 1979)
Stroudwater & Thames & Severn Canals Towpath Guide by M. Handford & D. Viner (Alan Sutton, 1984)
LMS Engine Sheds Vol. 2 by C. Hawkins & G. Reeve (Wild Swan Publications, 1981)
Index to Local & Personal Acts (HMSO, 1949)
Thames & Severn Canal by H. Household (David & Charles, 1969)
The Rise & Fall of the Severn Bridge by R. Huxley (Alan Sutton, 1984)
Industrial Locomotives of Central Southern England (Industrial Railway Society, 1981)
Twenty Years History of Stroud 1870 to 1890 by J. Libby
Biographical Dictionary of Railway Engineers by J. Marshall (David & Charles, 1978)
Nailsworth, The Official Guide by M.E.H. Mills
Severn & Wye Railway by H.W. Parr (David & Charles, 1973)
History of Nailsworth 1500-1900 by A.B. Pavey-Smith
Severn & Wye Railway Vols. 1-3 by I. Pope, R. How & P. Karau (Wild Swan Publications 1983, 1985, 1988)
An Historical Survey of the Midland in Gloucestershire by P. Smith (OPC, 1985)
Stroud as it was by J. Tucker
Victoria County History: Gloucestershire (Oxford University Press)

Magazines and Newspapers:
Bath Chronicle, Bristol Times & Mirror, Citizen, Gloucester Journal, Model Railway News, Railway & Travel Monthly, Railway Magazine, Railway Observer, Stroud News & Journal, Swindon Advertiser.

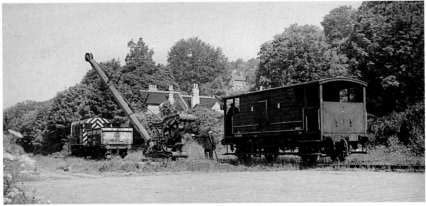

350 hp diesel shunter No. D3994 at Nailsworth with the last train on 1st June, 1966.

D. Payne